D0852961

A Closer Look at Dr. Laura

A Closer Look at Dr. Laura

Tom Allen

HORIZON BOOKS
A division of Christian Publications
CAMP HILL, PENNSYLVANIA

Horizon Books
A division of Christian Publications
3825 Hartzdale Drive, Camp Hill, PA 17011
www.cpi-horizon.com

ISBN: 0-88965-159-0
© 1998 by Christian Publications, Inc.
All rights reserved.
Printed in the United States of America

98 99 00 01 02   5 4 3 2 1

Cover photo by Blake Little

Unless otherwise indicated,
Scripture taken from the HOLY BIBLE:
NEW INTERNATIONAL VERSION ®.
© 1973, 1978, 1984 by
the International Bible Society.
Used by permission
of Zondervan Bible Publishers.

Dedication

This book is dedicated to
my brother John.
He was my hero when I was a young boy
watching #80 play football for the
Mansfield Senior High Tygers.
Thirty-two years later,
he's still my hero.

Contents

Part 5: Sexual Mores

Part 6: Spirituality

Epilogue:

OVER THE LAST DECADE, as my own religious journey led me from secularism to Orthodox Judaism, my internationally syndicated radio program reflected that personal growth and the acceptance of God's words as the ultimate moral authority for my "preaching, teaching and nagging" about morals, values and ethics.

A number of people warned me that being open about my Judaism and invoking God's words might stimulate an anti-Semitic backlash. To the contrary! The most immediate and continuous support from my program came from the Christian lay and ordained religious community.

Several months ago, Tom Allen contacted me to say he was writing a book comparing my preaching, teaching and nagging to the Christian viewpoint. I was both flattered and a little wary.

A few members of the Christian clergy have expressed concern that I *ignore* the concept of grace (salvation through Jesus Christ) in my writing and my conversations with callers who want to change their behavior and resolve situations that cause them and others pain.

I am frankly always puzzled by this criticism since Judaism does not embrace the divinity of Jesus Christ, and therefore does not adhere to the teachings about grace. Nevertheless, as I wrote in my new book *The Ten Commandments—The Significance of God's Laws in Everyday Life*, "There is a commonality to the motivation of Jews and Christians to *love* and *obey* God: salvation."

There are differences in the perspective of how and what that salvation entails. Both Jews and Christians see God as "Savior." For Jews, the saving grace is our survival in spite of external oppression and enemies. For Christians, that saving grace is Christ's sacrifice to save each Christian's soul from its own *inner* tendency toward sin. In the Christian view, the world is redeemed as each individual's soul is saved through Jesus Christ. In the Jewish view, we are redeeming the world by our own efforts.

As I said in my book, whether by the covenant at Sinai or by Jesus' resurrection, we are all charged, through a sense of duty and gratitude, to demostrate appreciation of God's saving grace through the way we *act*. The quality and character of how Jews and Christians lead their lives becomes the ongoing *visible* recognition of God's presence and truth.

I have always been encouraged by the strong and touching support I have received from the Christian community for my program as well as for my personal religious growth. It proves that people sincere about their love and awe of God are ultimately of one mind.

I believe that Tom Allen has attempted to be fair to my religious views and to what I have tried to accomplish on my radio program, which is to bring awareness and hopefully, acceptance, of the ultimate, eternal and universal morality of God and of our accountability to Him.

I have not bothered to quibble about a few points of contention because I respect Mr. Allen's right to his own opinion and perspective. While Mr. Allen and I may not always agree, I am pleased to say we share a mutual respect and admiration. He is a decent and sincere man, a religious man, and I am ultimately complimented that he chose to write this book.

I take the existence of the book as an acknowledgment that the good I am trying to do is of value to those for whom the sacred and the holy is central to a meaningful life. Thank you!

Warmly,
Dr. Laura Schlessinger
AKA: Her Kid's Mom
September 28, 1998

Acknowledgments

I wish to thank my wife, *Arliss,* and my daughters, *Andrea* and *Amanda,* for their patience with me during this project. Almost every day, they have heard me say, "You won't believe what happened on *The Dr. Laura Show* today!" The lifestyle of a writer is sometimes a bit odd, and I do appreciate their kindness and understanding.

Special thanks to

Dr. Laura Schlessinger for two things: First, graciously consenting to a personal interview. Second, I am deeply grateful for the Foreword.

Keven Bellows, Dr. Laura's publicist, who was particularly helpful in arranging our meeting. The staff treated my wife and me like royalty, and we are grateful. It was a real privilege to meet Dr. Laura and the wonderful people who surround her.

K. Neill Foster, who approached me about writing my first book back in 1978. I thought he was joking. Twenty years and seven books later, it is clear to me that he was not joking. He has consistently prodded me to be and become the best writer that God intended for me to be and become. And, at one particularly trying time in my career, he called with words of assurance that are still with me today.

The Ultimate Scrutiny

SOME WRITING ASSIGNMENTS ARE boring. Some are exciting. This one was intriguing.

When Dr. K. Neill Foster, President/Publisher of Christian Publications, Inc., called me in February, 1998 with this idea, my curiosity was immediately aroused.

A Closer Look at Dr. Laura . . . interesting . . . very interesting.

I had heard Dr. Laura Schlessinger on KSTP radio in the Minneapolis metropolitan area. I can remember telling my wife one day, "You've just got to hear this woman on the radio!" I was stunned by her fearless attack on immorality and irresponsibility. It was remarkable to hear someone on a secular talk show insist on sexual relationships only within the bond of marriage. She told *Leadership Journal*: "I have a secular show that's getting people religious. Who would have guessed?"[1] I just had to ask, "Who is this woman?!"

On July 13, 1998, my wife and I sat down with Dr. Laura for a personal interview at her studio in Sherman Oaks, California. Her publicist, Keven Bellows, greeted us, gave us lunch and took us to the studio where we observed a live production of *The Dr. Laura Show*.

Faxes steadily poured in the whole time we were there. *So that's where my faxes arrived,* I thought to myself. Phone lines were flickering—all the lines were always flickering. Staff members were moving quietly in and out. Notes were being passed into the soundproof booth. Never a dull moment.

Carolyn Holt, Dr. Laura's efficient call- screener, was punching buttons and asking a simple question: "What is the moral idea you're struggling with that you need Dr. Laura's input on?" She would patiently steer the callers in the direction of the show's intended purpose, but some just didn't want to go there. A polite goodbye and on to the next caller.

Through the glass, with his back to us, was Dan Mandis working his magic as the engineer/music orchestrator. He cues up the music that follows commercial breaks, and he has an uncanny ability to select tunes that relate to the most recent caller's moral dilemma. Though the music is most often upbeat, Dan quickly adapts to the somber mood of any situations that are just plain sad.

And there she was, facing us, at the back of the wall—dressed in her favorite red: Dr. Laura Schlessinger. After listening for many months, it was hard for me to believe that we were actually there in the studio with the Queen of Talk Radio. As I suspected, she was intense and animated. True to her Italian heritage, she spoke not just with her mouth, but with her hands, her facial expressions and her eyes.

Dr. Laura was very kind and straightforward during the interview. We knew within minutes that we were in the presence of someone who had a very charismatic personality, incredible wit and enough charm to fill the room. We were able to deal with difficult areas of controversy with relative ease and mutual respect.

2

For the past several months, I have researched the answer to questions such as: "On what is her sense of morality based?" and "How did she become so successful?" The reader will find the answers to these inquiries. But the question which forms the thesis for this book is a very simple one: "How does Dr. Laura line up with the Bible?"

On *The Late, Late Show* with Tom Snyder, Dr. Schlessinger defined her standards as "biblical": "I'm presenting standards like they're mine! I mean, you know—they're biblical! I'm reiterating them."[2]

She says of her program: "My values are an oasis in the middle of a moral nothingness. . . . I'm here to hold up a light and point a way."[3]

So, are her standards and values biblical? Just which way does she point?

These are vital questions because we are dealing with a celebrity who is being heard by millions of people each day. Her views and opinions often take the place of those of the priest and the pastor for the majority—those who do not attend church regularly. She is becoming somewhat of a spiritual guru for multiplied thousands of men and women in North America.

I want to explore this matter fairly and carefully. We will look at several major issues which Dr. Laura addresses on the radio and in her books, newspaper columns, magazines and web pages. Then we will examine each one in the light of the Bible.

Let me hasten to point out my definition of "the Bible." As an evangelical Christian, I am referring to both the Old and New Testaments in their entirety. In fairness and in contrast, it should be noted that Dr. Laura's Bible, as a devout Jew, is primarily the Torah—the five books of Moses. This is a crucial distinction. As an Orthodox Jew, Dr. Schlessinger's views are consistent with what she has learned from Judaism. I will be presenting an outlook that is consistent with my heritage as a Christian. And this will lead to very different conclusions on some issues.

Quite obviously, this is not a "trash Dr. Laura" book. I have enormous respect for her. Preparing this manuscript has been fun. It has also been a personal blessing in that I have learned some valuable things for my own spiritual growth.

But eventually, all people, regardless of their place in this world, must be accountable to the Word of God. This includes Dr. Laura—and me.

Join me in the journey. This is a fascinating woman with some very strong and colorful opinions. We shall soon see how her views stand up to the scrutiny of Scripture in both the Old and New Testaments.

It is the ultimate scrutiny.

Tom Allen
August, 1998

Meet Dr. Laura

Dr. Laura Schlessinger is, in some ways, a prophetess for our times. Funny and forthright. Never boring. Small of stature, big with boldness.

She has courageously challenged the many years of meaningless and impotent psychobabble that has been spewed over the airwaves into our North American culture. Because of her fearless use of moral absolutes to answer the questions of our time, she is invariably loved or hated.

I invite you now to meet Dr. Laura.

*"Lew, I'm a priest and my mission is
to help God perfect the world."*
—Dr. Laura

Good Things Come in
Small Packages

SHE IS ONLY FIVE feet, three inches tall. In February of 1998 she announced that even her twelve-year-old-son, Deryk, had become taller than Mom. But Dr. Laura Schlessinger packs a lot of charm, wit and wisdom into such a small physique. And if anyone thinks that he or she can take advantage of her, be warned: She attained her black belt in Hapkido karate in 1992!

"Dr. Laura," as she is affectionately known to her listeners, was born in 1947 in Brooklyn, New York. Her father, Monroe Schlessinger, was a Jew who fought in Northern Italy in World War II. Her mother was Yolanda Ceccovini, Monroe's Italian Catholic war bride. Raised without religion by a Jewish father and a Catholic mother who argued frequently, her childhood, she says, was not a happy one, and she often felt lost.[1]

But coming from "a mixed-religion marriage, she learned early about surviving bitter and petty prejudices . . . she grew to accept diversity of thought, opinion, and practice."[2] "My parents were pretty focused on 'right and wrong'—so I had early training on being concerned with correct behaviors," she says. "However, since the framework was not religious . . . it left itself open to interpretation, circumstance, and rationalization when I became a young adult on my own."[3]

Attending college during the late '60s, Laura Schlessinger was at first captivated by the original agenda of the feminist movement: equal pay for equal work. However, she later became enraged by the shift in focus. Though she celebrated the progress in law and societal action gained by this struggle, she also noted a certain loss for women—the notion of their specialness with respect to their unique position in the cycle of "new life."[4]

Dr. Schlessinger is well educated. She received her B.S. in Biology and a Ph.D. from the Physiology Department of the Medical School of Columbia University in New York. She also received her Post Doctoral Certification in Marriage and Family Therapy from the University of Southern California Human Relations Department in Los Angeles. Dr. Laura is licensed in the State of California as a marriage, family and child counselor, as well as being credentialed in hypnosis and sex therapy.

She taught as a member of the biological sciences faculty of the University of Southern California for five years, and she served on the graduate psychology faculty of Pepperdine University for eight years. Dr. Schlessinger has also been a guest lecturer at the University of California Los Angeles and the University of California Irvine Extension.

Some psychologists dismiss Dr. Laura on the grounds that her Ph.D. is in physiology rather than psychology. But it is quite obvious that she has carefully augmented her Ph.D. with more education, teaching roles and job experiences that more than qualify her for the task of radio psychologist. She is careful to not refer to herself as a "psychologist."

The Dr. Laura Show

This educational and professorial background of Laura Schlessinger opened doors of opportunity with her medium-of-choice—radio. She began with guest appearances on KABC Radio in Los Angeles. She then hosted her own show on KWIZ Radio in Santa Ana, California. She joined KFI-AM (Los Angeles) in 1990. With her radio talk show demanding more and more of her time, Dr. Laura gave up her private practice in 1993. *The Dr. Laura Show* went nationwide in syndication in 1994. She broadcasts five days a week, three hours a day from Premiere Radio Networks in the San Fernando Valley.

Just how successful is this radio talk show?

On September 10, 1997, Jacor Communications paid $71.5 million cash for *The Dr. Laura Show*. According to estimates by *Talkers* magazine, in 1998 Dr. Schlessinger surpassed Rush Limbaugh as the most listened-to person on the airwaves.[5] Tom Snyder introduced Dr. Laura on *The Late, Late Show* as "the most listened-to voice on coast-to-coast radio."[6] Approximately 20 million people listen weekly on over 450 stations in the United States and Canada, and the program can now be heard worldwide on the Armed Forces Radio Network. But here's the truly incredible statistic: AT&T estimates that 60,000 callers try to reach her program at 1-800-DRLAURA every day! This works out to be 333 calls per minute over the course of the three-hour show!

Dr. Schlessinger is quick to point out that the show is even more for the listeners than it is for the callers:

> I do the call for the listener. I have given up feeling compelled to change the caller. I can help so many, many more people that way. There are listeners out there identifying with each call, going, "Oh. That's me." If the caller gets it, that's icing.[7]

9

Because she comes across as a highly credible professional with the added advantage of a good sense of humor, Dr. Laura is sought after nationally by radio and television talk shows. She has appeared on *Oprah, Donahue, Entertainment Tonight, Geraldo, The John Davison Show, The Tom Snyder Show, Merv Griffin, Love/Sex/'n'/Rock 'n' Roll, Alive and Well, Breakaway, Fritz, Hour Magazine, Meet the Press, This Week with Sam Donaldson and Cokie Roberts, Larry King Live!* and others. Televangelist Robert Schuller, host of *Hour of Power*, has turned over his pulpit to her more than once.

Dr. Laura's Mission

Dr. Schlessinger was watching a PBS documentary about the Holocaust with her son Deryk when he was six years old. Naked mothers and children lined up to be executed. Deryk could not help but ask who those people were. Without even thinking, his mother blurted out, "Those are our people!" This was the life-changing moment in which she began to really think of herself as a Jew.

With characteristic aggression and energy, she dove into Jewish texts. One day, while reading in Genesis about the covenant between God and man, something clicked. It was an epiphany of sorts. Her life purpose suddenly and dramatically became clear: "I ran downstairs and yelled, 'Lew, I'm a priest and my mission is to help God perfect the world.' " [8]

This was in many ways "classic Dr. Laura"—a blend of audacity, excitement and genuine compassion. It was no doubt the recipe that led her to become the most popular woman on radio.

Not surprisingly, the stated purpose for her talk show is, in her own words, "to get people to be profoundly, deeply happy instead of just giddy for a moment."[9] Dr. Schlessinger believes she knows how to make that happen. And she feels that this is also the reason why her program has become so very popular.

Human beings are too complex to be categorized as just another animal, according to Dr. Laura. That complexity includes our sense of morality. Take away this element, and men and women become no more than termites seeking survival and gratification at all costs and at every moment. But with our built-in moral compass, we can and should transcend baser instincts and learned response. She says: "I started talking about honor, integrity, and ethics in tandem with the more traditional psychological approach and BANG!!! My radio program took off and became an international phenomenon."[10]

Though sometimes anathema to the psychological establishment, Dr. Schlessinger's approach to people's everyday problems has taken the country by storm. The purely psychology-oriented talk shows have faded away. She has utterly refuted her critics who insist that feelings must reign supreme and values must be considered relative. Dr. Laura is adamant: Her show is about moral health—not mental health.

The Making of Many Books, the Receiving of Many Awards

Dr. Laura Schlessinger also writes a nationally syndicated newspaper column and has her own web site. (In the spring of 1997, http://www.drlaura.com crashed when 310,000 people hit the web site at once!) She also has a monthly magazine. And she is the author of three best-selling books: *Ten Stupid Things Women Do to Mess Up Their Lives* (1994), *How Could You Do That?!* (1996) and *Ten Stupid Things Men Do to Mess Up Their Lives* (1997).

Each of these books is largely based on both the triumphant and tragic tales of those who have written, faxed and called in to her talk show. Dr. Laura has a wealth of material provided daily by the real-life dramas of those who dare to place their problems under the scrutiny of her x-ray vision into the human heart.

Her fourth book, released in September, 1998, is entitled, *The Ten Commandments: The Significance of God's Law in Everyday Life.* Cowritten with Rabbi Stewart Vogel, spiritual leader of Temple Aliyah in Woodland Hills, California, it focuses on the teachings of the commandments and their contemporary relevance. The first printing of 250,000 has been matched by a $250,000 promotional budget complete with a sixteen-city satellite TV tour and media appearances in New York City and Los Angeles.

Dr. Schlessinger has also received numerous awards. A few samples:

- In 1997, she was the first woman to be the recipient of the Marconi award, the top prize of the radio industry.
- On April 16, 1998, she received the Genie Award from the Southern California Chapter of American Women in Radio and Television (AWRT). This honor is given for outstanding talent in the field of radio.
- On June 4, 1998, in Garden Grove, California, she received the first Crystal Cathedral Academy Award for promoting family values in the media.

Funny Lady

Throughout the research process, I discovered that Dr. Schlessinger has an excellent sense of humor which she uses in combination with her keen sense of timing. Listen in on her conversation with Leonora and then Debby:

> LEONORA: I'm kinda hurt and disappointed. I met a guy at work and I've been dating him one month and it's clear that he drinks a lot. What do you think is his potential?

DR. LAURA: Potential for what? Drunk-driving arrests?

DEBBY: I met a man three months ago—we've had a few dates. I found out he's been involved in a shooting. Should I stay?

DR. LAURA: Only after watching Bonnie and Clyde for wardrobe suggestions.[11]

Suzy called to say that her husband is a hopeless alcoholic who refuses to get help. "What if I can't find another man?" she asked. Dr. Laura's response: "I guess it would be the end of the world, gravity would cease and the entropy of the universe would go for broke."[12]

Our resident talk show host doesn't have much patience with men and women who date or marry those who are ridiculously older or younger: "When a forty-seven-year-old man says he has a lot in common with a twenty-three-year-old girl, it means he's voluntarily retarded."[13]

Sarcasm is one of her best weapons in an impressive, rapid-fire verbal arsenal. Thirty-one-year-old Brett and his unmarried live-in girlfriend Sunny called *The Dr. Laura Show*. Sunny said that their lives would be idyllic "if it weren't for the fact that Brett goes out drinking with his buddies and, without calling home, stays out late instead of coming home." Brett protested that she was obviously too controlling: "I don't do it as often as she says."

When hit head-on with Dr. Laura's announcement that Brett has a drinking problem, surprisingly it was not Brett who was first to deny it. Sunny defended him by saying, "Well, oh-h-h, it's not that bad. If he would just stop doing that stuff, everything would be fine." Dr. Schlessinger quickly retorted, "And if it ever rained enough in the Sahara, you could plant tomatoes."[14]

Dr. Laura was the focus of Capitol Research Center's Culture Watch in May, 1997. In an article entitled "How Did Radio's Dr.

Laura Get Herself Compared to St. Thomas Aquinas?," Philip V. Brennan, Jr. highlighted her humor with this story: "So when a caller said he discovered that his wife was playing around, and that he had just learned she had been married five times before joining him in wedded bliss, Dr. Laura asked: 'How long had you known her before you got married . . . how many minutes?' "[15]

This talk show celebrity is uncanny in her ability to play off of the word pictures painted by her callers. Jean, fifty-four, started her conversation by telling Dr. Laura that she was "facing something that I'd just rather bury my head in the sand about. . . ." Without missing a beat, the doctor responded, "Yeah, Jean, but remember which end is sticking up in the air when you do that!"[16]

If it is true that a well-developed sense of humor is usually a sign of higher intelligence, then my guess is that Dr. Laura Schlessinger has a very high IQ. I found myself both quietly smiling and laughing out loud as I listened to her on the radio and read her books, articles, newspaper columns and newsletters.

Up Close and Personal

At the end of the paperback version of *Ten Stupid Things Women Do to Mess Up Their Lives,* there are some candid remarks about difficulties Dr. Laura has had to cope with in her personal life:

> She was married once before, for two years in her middle twenties, for all the wrong reasons highlighted in this book: fears of autonomy, issues of aloneness impacting on identity, etc. During her last year working on this book, her house burned down; eight months later, her husband was in cardiac intensive care for three weeks. . . . From her greatest depths she found the courage and energy

to continue in spite of the terrors that threatened
and contributed terrible anxiety and sadness.[17]

By her own admission, Dr. Schlessinger has found a source
of inner strength in her religion. She always identified with
the Jewish roots that came from her father's side of the family. She converted to Orthodox Judaism in 1996. Then, in
May, 1998, along with her husband Lew and son Deryk, Dr.
Laura converted to Conservative Judaism. Dr. Laura believes
that this is the pathway to meaning. Religious values, like
cooperation, sacrifice, compassion and love provide a road to
God. Motherhood also played a big role in reigniting her
spiritual curiosity:

> The experience of becoming a mother created in me a
> desire to discover a context for the new and very deep
> feelings I had for my son. In my study of religion, I ex-
> perienced a deep kinship with Judaism, the religion of
> my father, and all of us have now converted. Our de-
> votion to Judaism has enriched our family life immea-
> surably.[18]

Dr. Schlessinger was largely ignored by Jews and rabbis for the
first eighteen months after her talk show went national. Then
something happened at a conference of Conservative and Reform
rabbis which changed everything. The Conservative and Reform
rabbis decided that unmarried sex was OK as long as everybody
was up-front about it. At that same time, the Pope was reaffirm-
ing the fact that the rules in this regard for Catholics would not be
changing.

Dr. Laura took to the airwaves with this confrontational
comment:

> I am delighted that the Pope is on the cover of
> TIME as man of the year. He is one of the few
> people who maintains a value system that doesn't
> cater to whim and desire and change with the
> times. That takes guts which the rabbinical
> council didn't have.[19]

Shortly after taking this stand, she began hearing from lots of Jews! She is now dearly loved and embraced by the Jewish community.

Dr. Schlessinger is happily married to Dr. Lew Bishop, who manages her career and shares all the child-rearing experiences with their son, Deryk. She refers to her boy as "the best work of my life."[20] In an article entitled "What Is a Well-Lived Life?" for *Parade magazine*, Dr. Schlessinger reveals her deep affection for her husband, child and their family life together:

> Life with Deryk and Lew has taught me that the only
> balance worth worrying about is the balance between
> our investment in the material world and our invest-
> ment in our spiritual and emotional health. I've often
> been told I could make a lot more money if I would
> make more public appearances, travel more. But then
> I'd get to spend a lot less time with my family, and
> there just isn't enough money in the universe to make
> that appealing![21]

Dr. Laura is a very active woman with a wide variety of interests. Along with her former passion for karate, she is a "trekkie"
(someone who loves the *Star Trek* series). She collects unusual tea-
kettles and porcelain flowers. The doctor is also a powerboat en-
thusiast, weight lifter, power walker and mediocre (her
description) but enthusiastic tennis player.[22] She recently took

singing lessons, but warned her instructor that she would be his Waterloo. Evidently, after several months, the music teacher reluctantly agreed with her self-assessment.

"Singing will not be in my future," she said.[23]

*"She inspires devotion . . . and outrage . . .
but never indifference."*
—Joannie M. Schrof[1]

A Prophetess without Honor

IN THE LIGHT OF what I have written in chapter 1, one might wonder how anyone could make derogatory statements about a woman who has given her life to raise the standard of morality and make this world a better place. But that is precisely the problem for many of her critics. In a society that has made a religion out of situational ethics and mocked the reality of moral absolutes, Dr. Laura Schlessinger becomes a dangerous person.

There seems to be no middle ground here. Those who love her tend to do so wholeheartedly. And her critics are radical in their disdain for her. Or, as *U.S. News & World Report* put it, "Her detractors say she's a self-righteous prude capitalizing on shock-jock techniques."[2] There is even a web page on the Internet entitled "The I Hate (Intensely Dislike) Dr. Laura Schlessinger Page."

Consider a few of the issues for which she has been criticized.

A Rigid Style

Margaret Wente, columnist in the *Globe and Mail* (Toronto, Ontario, Canada), blasts Dr. Laura for her caustic approach:

Dr. Laura does not feel your pain. She believes in shaming people into right action . . . badgers her callers for having too much self-indulgence . . . likes to call them wimps and drunks, doormats and dustmops. She's been called the therapeutic equivalent of Rush Limbaugh, the right-wing ranter whom she now rivals in popularity. She is a moral absolutist and an anti-feminist. . . . And she thinks she's infallible.[3]

U.S. News & World Report writer Amy Bernstein wrote about "Dr. Laura's 'Moral Health Show' ":

She introduces herself on air as "my kid's mom." But Laura Schlessinger is no mild-mannered mother next door. This radio talk-show host is as outraged as Rush Limbaugh and as outspoken as G. Gordon Liddy—two leading voices of the conservative revolution. "Dr. Laura" is the personal, non-political side of that revolution, a therapist who rails against anything-goes mores.[4]

Doris Quan wrote the following critique for MSNBC:

Is she rude or just refreshingly blunt? Either way, there's no doubt that Dr. Laura Schlessinger, the Love Doctor, has filled an emotional void for millions of Americans. Dr. Laura responds to people's questions with a moralistic approach, which means no sympathy for adulterers, abusers, or addicts. She cuts people off, tells them they're "screwed" or "selfish." This is confrontational counseling—enough to make some listeners wince with pathos for the caller who actually got through.[5]

As I was writing this book, I spoke with my travel agent in Colorado Springs. She was asking me about my latest writing project. When I told her that the title was *A Closer Look at Dr. Laura,* she started to chuckle. Anxious to explore that reaction, I probed a bit. Finally, she came out with it. "I feel sorry for the poor folks that are able to talk to her. She can be pretty rough!"

Kristin Tillotson, writing an article entitled "Doctor, Heal Thyself" for the *Minneapolis Star Tribune,* made some caustic observations in an open letter to Dr. Laura. She mentioned the fact that someone who can "dish it out" should also be able to "take it." Ms. Tillotson then launched into a New Year's resolution for Dr. Laura to follow: "Here it is, Job One for '98: Reshuffle your deck of moral absolutes so that hearts, not clubs, are the trump suit, and compassion, not righteousness is the ace. . . . I'm not taking your basic ideology to task; it's your rigid style that needs sandpaper."

Ms. Tillotson proceeds to point out the convenient anonymity which a radio talk show offers. It is possible to get close to someone else's discomfort or disaster without actually being there. It is possible to listen in the privacy of one's home or car as judgment is meted out. Sometimes the advice that is offered seems like the quick fix of a sugar high, says Tillotson. She concludes her critique with this: "You won't be remembered for good advice, but for your grating tone. Until you temper your rushes to judgment with a dash of humanity, you have no business posing as a good Samaritan. The hand that helps is not the hand that spanks."[6]

Ms. Tillotson reported ten days later that 125 people had e-mailed responses to her "Doctor, Heal Thyself!" column. The comments were 9-to-1 in her favor.[7]

A Flaw in the Ointment

Some complain that the format itself (talk radio) is blemished. Michael Skube, writing in the *Atlanta Journal Constitution,* says:

> I agree with her half of the time, but there's a flaw in the format. You can't solve a real problem in two minutes. But a lot of people who call in don't have real problems. The few who do have serious problems, she can't give them the time they need.[8]

Evidently, many of Dr. Laura's critics in psychological circles agree with this assessment. They consider it to be fast-food advice. Dr. Lilli Friedland, onetime president of the media-psychology division of the American Psychological Association, says that Schlessinger:

> gives a lot of people what they want. In our culture people want fast answers and don't want to work hard to make wise choices. . . . In order to make a clinical intervention, a psychologist has to know the history of an individual. A five-minute introduction is not enough on which to base a diagnosis.[9]

But at least one doctor defends the call-in talk show. Dr. Irwin Schussler of Psychiatric Associates in Fort Worth, Texas, gives it a positive spin. He says that people are often more comfortable phoning in their questions than consulting face-to-face. This is especially true if the person has not had any one-on-one dealings with a psychologist or psychiatrist and has no idea what to expect:

> Call-in talk shows can be a welcome avenue to get some basic questions answered anonymously. The telephone is

a very safe way to communicate, and I think it does a whole lot for demystifying and desensitizing mental health issues. . . . It's also a lot less expensive than individual counseling.[10]

Screwed, Etc.

Dr. Laura has also been criticized for using crass language. Listen to this caller:

> I admire your moral and religious values and applaud your views with respect to stay-at-home mothers and being faithful to the vows. There is something that bothers me though. That is the use of words and phrases that are used to get through to some of your callers. Words like "screwed, knocked up," etc., leave me cold. While on the other hand, you are trying to make your audience rise to high moral standards, you then lower yourself by that way of speaking.[11]

Dr. Schlessinger's defense of her usage of words is compelling:

> I'm not going to use "lovemaking" when people are screwing around. Lovemaking is in a marital covenant. Anything other than that is screwing around. So, I use words to describe the activity, and if the activity happens within a covenant, then it has sacred words attached to it. If the activity happens outside of a covenant, then they [sic] have profane words. . . . So we are real clear on that. It's intentional.[12]

23

Some listeners would probably agree with the sentiment of an e-mail critique about the use of other types of language by Dr. Laura. She often uses the term "God" when she is not referring to Him, and this would fit the definition of "taking God's name in vain" for some people. She also uses four-letter words (the "d____" word and the "h____" word), along with the "b____" word to describe certain types of women. The critic summarized her thoughts with this statement: "If she is going to be a 'moral compass' she needs to be one, and that includes using clean words. . . . People who think she is the voice of how to live right will think cussing is O.K."[13]

The Shrinks Speak Out

How is Dr. Laura Schlessinger viewed among psychologists? Most of them are quick to point out that the "Dr." in Dr. Laura has to do with physiology—not psychology. This leads Dr. Lilli Friedland to say: "Her information is not the kind that a psychologist gives. We're supposed to guide people, not lead them."[14]

Dr. Victoria Lee is a San Francisco psychologist who has researched the phenomenon of radio therapists. She contends that Dr. Schlessinger is too swift to interject her own opinions: "Real therapy doesn't make good entertainment. There would be too many silences. Instead of insisting on their [sic] own viewpoint, a good therapist asks a lot of questions."[15]

A popular Fort Worth psychologist, Dr. David Welsh, admits that he both applauds and deplores Dr. Laura. He is most concerned with the way this talk radio host plays fast and loose with the boundaries between health professional and moral adviser:

> To some extent, Dr. Laura represents a contemporary version of the public pillory. It's a sick, voyeuristic thing to see someone laid bare and humiliated in pub-

lic. It appeals to our prurient interests. I've heard her take people struggling with very hard issues—and just crucify them. . . . It's entertaining. It's ambush journalism. We are voyeurs driving by an accident site and slowing down to take in all the gory details.[16]

However, Dr. Welsh concedes that Dr. Laura's emphasis on character is touching a nerve in a culture which sorely needs to be touched:

This is sometimes an amoral, valueless society we live in. She speaks out very publicly about making decisions on the basis of moral principle as opposed to what feels good. I think we in the mental health field have sometimes erred in advising people to do what feels good, what provides them the most self-esteem and happiness. She's kind of a voice in the wilderness.[17]

Welsh applauds Dr. Laura for her willingness to point people to further counseling for some problems. And she balances this by warning others that too much therapy can become self-defeating by rummaging around childhood experiences and rehashing the past over and over. Dr. Welsh likes the way that Dr. Schlessinger simply will not allow people to make themselves victims.

One psychotherapist, Dr. Marilyn Anderson, says that Dr. Schlessinger's brusque approach wears thin pretty quickly with her. But she admits that the radio doctor has good information: "She reminds me of Dr. Albert Ellis, a writer and fairly well-known professor of psychology. His approach is 'I'm going to tell you the way it is, and I don't give a d——if you like it or not.' "[18]

As director of information and referral for the Mental Health Association of Tarrant County, Texas, Mike Hawkins often takes calls from people struggling to take charge of their lives. He maintains an extensive list of all sorts of referrals. His thoughts on the queen of talk radio: "I think Dr. Laura has some pretty practical-type advice for folks. She really zeroes in on some of the problems of everyday life."[19]

Dr. William Doherty, a Minnesota therapist, wrote a book in 1995 entitled *Soul Searching: Why Psychotherapy Must Promote Moral Responsibility.* He is troubled by his profession, which he says must stop practicing "moral lobotomy." In support of Dr. Schlessinger's tough stand against the "feel-good" therapies utilized by many counselors, he says: "Therapy that focuses only on what feels good to me is bankrupt. Happiness is founded on some measure of being good and useful to others."[20]

Dr. Schlessinger vs. Dr. Browne

The longest-running psychologist on network radio is Dr. Joy Browne. She has been a corporate research psychologist, a university professor and a therapist in private practice. A native of New Orleans, Dr. Browne began her radio career in Boston and moved on to San Francisco (KGO and KCBS) and then to WABC, New York. Since 1986, she has been with ABC Talk Radio Network in New York.

Oprah Winfrey, Phil Donahue and Joan Rivers have used Joy Browne as their resident psychologist, and this has given her national recognition. Her Ph.D. is in psychology. This sets her apart from Dr. Laura. But there is more that distinguishes Dr. Browne from Dr. Schlessinger. A promo for station WMC AM 790 made this statement in support of Joy Browne. It is an obvious allusion to Dr. Laura's abrupt style: "She [Dr. Browne] stresses heartfelt compassion and occasional 'tough love' rather than the value judgments and acidic ridicule her imitators offer."[21]

In response to an article contrasting Dr. Browne and Dr. Schlessinger on the Internet, one of Dr. Browne's fans wrote:

> Dr. Laura Schlessinger often says that her role is to "Preach, Teach and Nag." This is entirely different from Dr. Browne's "Problem Solving" approach. Personally, I find Dr. Laura to be judgmental, cold and often unrealistic. . . . I still don't understand her popularity compared to that of Browne's [sic]. Maybe listener's [sic] enjoy being slapped around and continuously told they are morally weak.[22]

No Excuse for Their Sin

In one of the most unpopular passages in the Gospels, Jesus warns His followers: " 'No servant is greater than his master.' If they persecuted me, they will persecute you also. . . . If I had not come and spoken to them, they would not be guilty of sin. Now, however, they have no excuse for their sin" (John 15:20, 22).

There is a sense in which Dr. Laura is being persecuted for the same reason alluded to here in John 15. Jesus exposed sin for what it truly was, and even those in the religious establishment found themselves in need of repentance. Those who turned from their evil ways loved and followed Christ. Those who didn't want to hear it hated Him and wanted to kill Him.

It is little wonder that one writer calls Dr. Schlessinger "a petite, blonde, latter-day version of Moses on the mountain" who "delivers her commandments every day from behind her microphone."[23] She has had the courage to challenge the reckless and rampant immorality disguised as amorality which plagues our world. People want to hear this: "Well, it's not really your fault! You just couldn't help yourself! Your moral failure (or hatred, lying, alcoholism, etc.) must be someone else's responsibility!" Dr. Laura's response to that kind of impotent cop-out has been boldly, brutally consistent: "You made the mess, and you will have to clean it up!"

The doctor had her own "mess" to clean up in October, 1998.

One-time mentor and former radio host, Bill Balance, seventy-nine, claimed that he had an affair with Dr. Laura in the mid 1970s. He had taken nude photos of her at that time and decided to post them on the Internet. Internet Entertainment Group said it paid Ballance "tens of thousands of dollars" for the "dirty dozen" pics. Dr. Schlessinger's legal team won a temporary court order to stop the photos from being posted, but it was lost on appeal on November 2, 1998.[24]

It would have been easy for Dr. Laura to blast this man from her past for cashing in at her expense. Her admiring listeners would have been incensed at Mr. Ballance's voyeuristic lack of values. But she maintained her dignity with her silence. And, in view of her recent "moral conversion," fan concensus was that she should not be held to things that happened more than two decades ago.

Those who claim that she is rigid are no doubt feeling the rub of her insistence on moral absolutes. As Rabbi Peter Grumbacher said it: "Maybe you and I want to reach through the radio and throttle her because she hits a raw nerve on more than one occasion?"[25]

In many ways it is easier to live in a culture that has no definite sense of right and wrong. We can all have our opinions, and no one is the final authority. But Dr. Laura makes a convincing case for getting back to the unchanging moral laws of God. And similar to Jesus, those who follow the good doctor's advice love her. The ones who reject her wisdom tend to renounce and dislike her too.

Though I understand and agree with some of her detractors in regard to her impatience and abrupt style, I radically disagree with Kristin Tillotson, quoted earlier in this chapter.

You're wrong, Ms. Tillotson. Sometimes the hand that helps *is* the hand that spanks.

Human Development

Dr. Laura has some interesting insights into the matter of human development. It all begins when a person decides to take personal responsibility for his or her actions. Upon this foundation can be built character, courage and conscience. And in this context, instant gratification loses much of its appeal.

"Our kids are imbued with victimology,
the new, American way of blame.
Adults and their kids routinely
explain their problems as victimization."
—Dr. Martin E.P. Seligman and Dr. Roger
Weissberg[1]

The Age of the Victim

WRITING IN HER BOOK, *Ten Stupid Things Women Do to Mess Up Their Lives,* Dr. Laura notes, "In The Age of the Victim, nothing is anybody's fault!"[2] She goes on to present a virtual boutique of excuses designed to allow people to marinate in their weaknesses:

- "I'm sick."
- "I'm codependent."
- "I'm addicted."
- "I was loved too much."
- "I was loved too little."
- "I was scarred by a dysfunctional past."

These are some of the ways people rationalize their self-destructive behavior. But where is the sense of personal responsibility? The doctor says: "Victimization status is the modern promised land of absolution from personal responsibility. Nobody is acknowledged to have free will or responsibility anymore. Everyone is the product of causation."[3]

She goes on to explain how she became rather opinionated with regard to the blame game. The doctor had a change of mind early in her career with regard to this critical question: "Why do people do what they do?" She says:

> I began my radio talk-program career simultaneously with my training in Marriage, Family, and Child Therapy. The training didn't exactly say that people were not at all responsible for their condition, but it did emphasize that external situations and internal angst provided an almost inexorable force that became explanation, if not excuse, for all the . . . destructive behaviors that messed up their lives.[4]

For this reason, Dr. Schlessinger's early on-air radio dialogues tended to focus on those insights that would offer clues to the origins of a caller's predicaments. She became quite skilled at moving her radio listeners toward an understanding of the various outside influences that made them behave in certain ways. Dr. Laura referred to things like unfinished developmental stages, unmet needs, experiences of loss, hurt or fear or abandonment by a parent. It had the appearance of a very neat package. But eventually, she decided, it was "too neat. It worried me."[5]

She became bothered by the notion that when bad things happen, this automatically predisposes someone to other problems. This seemed out-of-touch with reality to her. Besides, all people to whom the same thing happened did not end up with the same type of quality of life. A radical change took place in Dr. Laura's approach. She no longer declared everyone to be the helpless victim of someone else's evil actions.

Frankly, this is one of the things that attracted me to her books and radio show. Like many others, I am tired of hearing so many excuses for why people do the stupid things they do. With some regrets for advice she'd given in the past, Dr. Laura says, "I switched my thinking from cause-effect to possible influence—as I worried just how great a role blaming something in the past and reverence for victimhood was functioning to help people stay stuck."[6]

"I'm only human. . . ."

One of Dr. Schlessinger's pet peeves centers around callers who protest that they are "only human":

> *Only* human? As if one's humanness were a blueprint for instinctive, reflexive reactions to situations, like the rest of the animal kingdom. I see being "human" as the unique opportunity to use our mind and will to act in ways that elevate us above the animal kingdom.[7]

Dr. Laura finds a good illustration of these clashing definitions of humanity in the classic film *The African Queen.* Humphey Bogart assumed the role of Charlie, the solitary soldier. He tried to invoke the "I'm only human" excuse in an attempt to explain his drunken stupor. But Rosie, a missionary played by Katharine Hepburn, would have none of it. She peered over her Bible with this retort: "We were put on this earth to rise above nature."[8]

"Addiction" and "Disease" Excuses

Someone wrote to Dr. Laura's question and answer newspaper column to report on some advice that Ann Landers had given. A couple had been married for twenty-five years. They finally decided to withdraw from his parents because they were "addicted" to alcohol. For too many years, he and his wife had been on call to stop the fights, pick them up, put them in bed and take them to the hospital after drunken falls or overmedication. The minister and social worker both supported them in throwing in the towel.

Ann Landers offered some shocking advice: "Instead of turning your backs on them, why not at least try once again to get them to seek the help they need?"[9] Landers pronounced the parents victims!

Dr. Laura was outraged with this response. She conceded that alcohol has an addictive quality that makes it difficult to stop drinking—but not impossible! She pointed out that the parents are not relieved of responsibility for their actions and moral obligations just because they choose to become inebriated. In Dr. Schlessinger's opinion, "these people are selfish and victimize everyone in their lives while they hide behind the excuse of 'disease' and blame everyone else for their problems."[10]

Dr. Laura received a large response to this column, but that was not the surprising aspect. The replies to her strong comments were 9-to-1 in agreement! She continues her castigation of what our culture calls "diseases" and "addictions" by addressing the real issue: "Acknowledging that you are basically the perpetrator of your mess of a life is admittedly very upsetting. But it is that very acknowledgment that gives you the power to change things. After all, what you can take away, you can give."[11]

I Am What I Choose to Do

Dr. Laura Schlessinger is a strong advocate of the fact that God has given us a free will. We can choose which way we want to go: "All sorts of political, psychological, social, and medical theories have been postulated to justify what people simply choose to do."[12]

According to the queen of talk radio, we can choose and alter our actions at will. We make conscious choices. We choose between options, but not all of those alternatives are created equal in terms of outcome or inherent value. Dr. Laura insists that we never lose the freedom and responsibility to make choices and then honor them.

She told *Leadership Journal:* "God left us with the will to choose, the freedom to choose, and we don't always choose right. Which is why we don't have heaven on earth."[13]

Dr. Schlessinger was interviewed by Cokie Roberts on ABC News' *This Week with Sam Donaldson and Cokie Roberts.* She was asked about two boys in Arkansas, ages eleven and thirteen, who murdered four students and one teacher at a middle school in March, 1998: "There is an intentionality in picking up guns and picking off kids . . . ultimately, they are absolutely responsible for their actions. They were premeditated—they knew exactly what they were doing. And since they were brought up hunting, they understood death."[14]

This statement is a huge departure from those of her colleagues. Many psychologists and psychiatrists would choose to blame: 1) society; 2) the family structure (or lack thereof); 3) a "genetic predisposition to violence"; 4) any combination of the above.

Lions and Lawyers and Lawsuits—Oh My!

Dr. Laura always takes time to note and celebrate those occasions when people take personal responsibility for their actions—even when they do bad things. She relates the story of a forty-year-old woman who was mauled by a mountain lion in a state park in 1994. Here's a big surprise: A lawyer was involved almost immediately with a lawsuit against the state for failing to maintain the mountain lion population! However, upon further consideration, the woman's husband decided to drop his $10,000 claim, stating: "Barbara and I have always taken responsibility for our own actions. Barbara chose to run in the wilds and, on a very long shot, did not come back. This is not really the fault of the state. In my opinion, people should take responsibility for themselves."[15]

According to *U.S. News & World Report,* our society is ready for this change of rules and roles in this blame game we've been endorsing. Taking responsibility for one's actions is gaining popularity:

> Polls show an increasing public impatience with excuses and a demand for accountability. . . . Even many therapists, crucial purveyors of American values, are emphasizing words like character and responsibility—and encouraging their clients and their colleagues to do the same.[16]

A Royal Response to Dr. Laura

Scripture is full of confirmations for Dr. Schlessinger's insistence on taking responsibility for one's actions. Indeed, Adam and Eve were judged for their unwillingness to own their sin in the Garden of Eden. This is where the whole "blame game" began. A friend of mine, Dr. Erwin Lutzer, says that when the first humans were caught in the act, "Adam blamed Eve—Eve blamed the serpent—and the serpent didn't have a leg to stand on!"

Perhaps the most dramatic example of the call to personal responsibility comes in the Old Testament story of Nathan the prophet and King David. David had a tryst with the lovely

Bathsheba, and she became pregnant. To cover up the affair, David put her husband Uriah in harm's way by sending him to the front lines "where the fighting is fiercest" (2 Samuel 11:15). King David got his wish. Uriah was quickly killed. David married Bathsheba. He thought it was a done deal.

"But the thing David had done displeased the LORD" (11:27). The prophet Nathan was commissioned by God to confront the king with his wickedness. God's messenger used the story of a poor man who had nothing except one little ewe lamb he had bought. The indigent man loved and cherished this lamb, and the animal became like a member of the family. His employer, a wealthy man, had a special guest for dinner and decided to butcher the poor man's ewe lamb even though he had plenty of other lambs to choose from. David "burned with anger" (12:5) as he thought how cruel this rich man had been. But Nathan suddenly got to the punch line: "You are the man!" (12:7).

I am convinced that King David was known as "a man after God's own heart" because of his response to the prophet's condemnation of his adultery and murder. Though he had committed terrible sins, he was willing to take responsibility for his actions. David's lowly repentance is found in Psalm 51:1-3:

> Have mercy on me, O God,
>   according to your unfailing love;
> according to your great compassion
>   blot out my transgressions.
> Wash away all my iniquity
>   and cleanse me from my sin.
> For I know my transgressions,
>   and my sin is always before me.

Note the intensely personal nature of this confession. The king was not blaming Bathsheba for her well-contoured body or for her bathing in public. He did not discuss something his parents did to him that made him more lustful than other men. David simply agreed with Nathan that he and he alone was the man responsible for both the adultery and the murder. No blaming. No hiding. No excuses. "I did it. Lives have been destroyed because of it. I was terribly wrong to do it. I am deeply sorry for it." God honors that kind of gut-wrenching honesty.

Our Own Evil Desires

The New Testament writer James weighs in on this issue of personal responsibility with regard to temptation:

> When tempted, no one should say, "God is tempting me." For God cannot be tempted by evil, nor does he tempt anyone; but each one is tempted when, by his own evil desire, he is dragged away and enticed. Then, after desire has conceived, it gives birth to sin; and sin, when it is full-grown, gives birth to death. (James 1:13-15)

This text emphasizes the fact that we are each subject to our "own evil desire." There are a variety of evil allurements. Some forms of wickedness will appeal to you, but not to me and vice versa. But in every case, we should take note of the perpetrator: It's me. It's you! Ultimately, we cannot blame anyone else for our response to temptation.

Judgment Day Accountability

This theme of personal responsibility is clearly stated in reference to our judgment before God someday. The apostle Paul has something important to say about the intensely personal nature of that judgment: "For we will all stand before God's judgment seat. . . . each of us will give an account of himself to God" (Romans 14:10, 12).

We will not give an account for our spouse, children, boss or friend. "Each of us." This is the ultimate sense in which we will be personally responsible for our own thoughts, words and deeds.

Competent to Counsel

Dr. Laura is most frequently criticized for her candid, machine-gun method for getting to the heart of the issue with people who call the show. But the real rub is most often a rebellious response to her insistence on people taking responsibility for their behaviors. Those of us involved in any kind of counseling work need to take notes on her approach.

It is safe to say that secular psychology has made deep inroads into the traditional biblical philosophy of counseling. Religious advisers spend many hours listening to people go on and on describing their childhood traumas, bad marital experiences and other macabre events of their past. Though there is a need for folks to talk about such things, we have often failed to ask the vital question that I hear Dr. Laura ask: "How are you responding to the difficulties you've been through?"

No one is responsible for the evil actions of someone else. The child molester, the wife beater, the adulterer—these people are responsible for their own reprehensible behavior. The victim of these sordid deeds is accountable only for his or her response. If he chooses the way of hatred, bitterness, retribution or imitation, there will be a price to pay for those reactions. If, however, he opts to love, forgive and treat others differently than he was treated, the reward will be commensurate.

Dr. Laura Schlessinger is biblically on target when she insists that we should stop blaming the world, the flesh and the devil for our bad behavior. I have not the slightest doubt that a fresh emphasis on the principle of personal responsibility from God's Word in our society would bring about a spiritual renewal throughout the land.

*"Never esteem anything as of advantage to you that will
make you break your word or lose your self-respect."*
—Marcus Aurelius[1]

When No One Else Is Looking

"To BE FULLY HUMAN and to benefit maximally from the
life experience, you must get back to the 3 C's: Character,
Courage, and Conscience."[2]

In the next three chapters, we want to look at the issues of
character, courage and conscience through the eyes of Dr.
Laura Schlessinger. Most of what she has to say about these
matters is found in her third book (in my judgment the best of
them all), *How Could You Do That?!*

Dr. Laura uses a familiar definition for the concept of character:
"what you are when no one else is looking."[3] A major news magazine states that "her confrontational, poke-at-the-conscience style
is closely tuned to a late 1990's revival of the old-fashioned notion
that how you behave says something about who you are."[4]

The doctor shares a poem by "author unknown" to under-
score this:

> I can never hide myself from me,
> I see what others may never see.
> I know what others may never   know,
> I can never fool myself and so . . .
> Whatever happens I want to be,
> Self-respecting & conscience free![5]

Dr. Laura tells a story from her own life which I think is an excellent example of her own sense of character. After her son, Deryk, was born, she was anxious to get back into radio. It seemed like an impossible dream. But then a small radio station near her home offered her a midday program. The wages were not nearly as adequate as her gratitude for the job. She could be with her son all morning. They could walk to the station, Deryk could stay at the play center while she was on the air, then they could walk home and have the afternoon and evening together.

It seemed like the ideal scenario. However, there was one catch: "The only request the station owner made is that I would not take time off his air to fill-in or audition on any other station."[6]

Guess what happened? Shortly after she agreed to this stipulation, the big talk station in town wanted her to audition. For years she had been waiting for this opportunity. It looked too good to pass up. But Dr. Laura had made a promise. How could she go back on her word and maintain her integrity? Her friends told her to forget her commitment and go for the bigger opportunity. It was an incredible temptation. She eventually called the larger radio station and declined.

They continued to pressure her, but the doctor held firm. Proud of herself for refusing to compromise her word, she summed up her experience with these poignant words: "I can assure you that integrity is its own reward if what you're seeking is spiritual peace, a quality life, and quality relationships."[7]

This is a powerful illustration of Dr. Laura's own commitment to character "when no one else was looking." She could have taken that bigger job with better pay. It's highly unlikely that we would have read an article entitled, "Dr. Laura Jilts Smaller Station for Big Bucks." Life would have gone on for that little station, and most people would have just assumed that Dr. Laura was climbing the ladder of success by making such a move.

But she had given her word. She had pledged not to fill in and not to audition. She kept that promise. She passed a key test of character. In her own words: "Life is often quite tough, challenging us to choose between seemingly esoteric, intangible ideals and getting goodies or good vibes right now. You have character when you most often choose ideals."[8]

Dr. Laura illustrates this with a caller named Tina who had a rude awakening. At twenty-two, she had been married for six months when she and her husband, Jack, went out for a most revealing dinner with three other couples. All the guys at the table had been at Jack's bachelor party. He had promised Tina that there would be no women or sex at that soiree—just drinking on his last night as a single man.

But now the truth about that fateful evening came out in living, lustful color. Jack's friends went on and on about how he enjoyed the services of the "entertainment dancer" who had been hired for the festivities. He had lied about his intentions for the party and then covered it up. Dr. Laura asked Tina what she was left with in the light of this embarrassing revelation: "I know that he lied to me before and after the fact, and that he had intimate sex with a complete stranger. I now see him as having little character and believe that I cannot trust him to resist impulses."[9]

Dr. Schlessinger highlighted the one important thing that Tina learned about Jack through this devastating discovery. In the battle between self-indulgence and self-sacrifice, Tina's husband would lean toward self-indulgence. She could no longer count on him to do the right thing. Jack would most likely not honor his commitments to her or others.

Leading with Character

On January 29, 1998, a public university fund-raiser in Fullerton, California, was conducted in honor of veteran newscaster Walter Cronkite. Dr. Laura was the keynote speaker that evening. She took the opportunity to make some mordant comments on the continuing sex scandal swirling around President Clinton in regard to the vital importance of character in leadership.

She was saddened by the disgusting media frenzy. But she was even more troubled by the preposterous reaction of many Americans. The attitude was: "Who cares what the President does in private? What really matters is how he does his job!" The shallowness and amorality of that mentality vexed Dr. Schlessinger:

> When people in positions of responsibility and power degrade their opportunity to lead by giving in to their personal weaknesses of lust, conquest, power, arrogance, ego or greed, they cease to set a good example. . . . It is essential that people in the public view and trust be models of what is most noble, moral, and holy in our potential as human beings.[10]

This was an unusually brave declaration in the context of the times in which it was stated. The press had been unwilling to make the connection between the private and public behavior of the President. Dr. Laura boldly reminded us all that there is a correlation. Leaders with character maintain integrity in both their public and private lives.

Character as Its Own Reward

Dr. Laura is realistic about the fact that those who choose to develop character and live according to Judeo-Christian ethical standards may not always feel like they are being adequately compensated for the sacrifices involved. Things like integrity, honor and honesty may not be instantly rewarded. In fact, she says, they could even be life-threatening in the case of someone who turns state's evidence. Conversely, the absence of these virtues does not always bring swift punishment or scorn. Evil people often gain both power and wealth. She summarizes with this potent epigram: "Therefore, morality must be its own reward."[11]

She illustrates this principle with the story of Tony. He was twenty-nine, single and on the verge of watching his career take off. If he could just focus his time, effort and resources, he would become very successful. And rich. But there was a problem. Two years earlier, his older sister and her husband were instantly killed in an accident. Tony's sister had taken the two children. Now, however, the ten- and thirteen-year-old kids had become too demanding in terms of space and finances. So they moved in with Tony.

It was not that Tony didn't feel sympathy for the plight of these orphaned children, but he sensed that this was his moment. Taking in these kids seemed to be about the worst thing that could happen to his career. Dr. Laura reduced reality to its essence by asking the perfect question: "If I could project you fifteen years into the future and you could look back at this time in your life, what would you want to see yourself having done?"[12]

Tony said the only thing left to say. He decided that he must continue to help the children.

A part of Tony's reward, according to Dr. Schlessinger, is the joy that will come in the future when he looks back at decisions which were based on good character: "Human beings can actually derive pleasure in the very act of resisting temptations, from not getting something, someone, or someplace the easy way."[13]

Joseph: Quite a Character

In the Old Testament, Jacob's son, Joseph, is the very epitome of the definition of character as described by Dr. Laura. His story begins in Genesis 37.

At the age of seventeen, Joseph had lofty dreams about his future as a leader. He made the mistake of sharing this with his older brothers—complete with the image of them bowing down to him. They were not amused. In a fit of jealous rage, they sold the wonder boy as a slave to Midianite merchants. The siblings went so far as to soak Joseph's clothes in goat's blood to make Jacob believe that Joseph had been mauled by a wild animal.

The Midianites, with Joseph in tow, traveled on to Egypt and sold him to Pharaoh's captain of the guard, Potiphar. His new Egyptian master was so impressed with Joseph that he put him in charge of his household and all that he owned. Because of Joseph's efficient management, according to Genesis 39:6, the only thing Potiphar had to be concerned with was the age-old question, "What's for dinner?"

Scripture indicates that Joseph was "well-built and handsome" (39:6). Potiphar's wife began to notice his striking good looks. She decided to test Joseph's character with an incredibly tempting offer:

> "Come to bed with me!"
>
> But he refused. "With me in charge," he told her, "my master does not concern himself with anything in the house; everything he owns he has entrusted to my care. No one is greater in this house than I am. My master has withheld nothing from me except you, because you are his wife. How then could I do such a wicked thing and sin against God?" And though she spoke to Joseph day after day, he refused to go to bed with her or even be with her.
>
> One day he went into the house to attend to his duties, and none of the household servants was inside. She caught him by his cloak and said, "Come to bed

with me!" But he left his cloak in her hand and ran out of the house. (Genesis 39:7-12)

There is significance in the phrase, "none of the household servants was inside." No one else was looking! Potiphar's wife thought she had finally caught Joseph in a scenario where he would succumb to the temptation—no witnesses. Day after day she had seductively employed the power of suggestion. Now she could catch him at a weak and private moment. The scene is reminiscent of the story of the adulteress in Proverbs:

> I noticed among the young men,
> a youth who lacked judgment.
> He was going down the street near her
> corner. . . .
> Then out came a woman to meet him,
> dressed like a prostitute and with crafty intent. . . .
> [S]he said . . .
> I looked for you and have found you! . . .
> Come, let's drink deep of love till morning;
> let's enjoy ourselves with love!
> My husband is not at home;
> he has gone on a long journey. . . .
> All at once he followed her
> like an ox going to the slaughter. . . .
> (7:7-8, 10, 13, 15, 18-19, 22)

However, Joseph was no ox. He refused this philandering woman's final plea, even when no one else was looking. He maintained his character before God and the captain's wife. And what reimbursement did he get for his strenuous efforts to deny himself the pleasure of her company? A raise in pay? An extra week of vacation? Not quite. Joseph was accused of rape.

Convicted. Sent to prison. Some reward! But once again, we see his character in action as he patiently waited to be vindicated.

That's exactly what God did for Joseph. The Lord enabled him to miraculously interpret dreams. Joseph became so renowned for this skill in prison that Pharaoh himself summoned him to translate his own troubled dreams. The king was so impressed with this ability that he made Joseph his chief of staff: "All my people are to submit to your orders. Only with respect to the throne will I be greater than you" (Genesis 41:40).

I've always wondered how Potiphar and his wife took this news.

Eventually, Joseph's brothers were forced by a famine to go to Egypt in search of grain. And just who do you think was the one to whom Pharaoh had entrusted his grain distribution program? Sure enough—Joseph! The brothers would meet again! And they would bow down in his presence!

One question remained: What kind of leader had Joseph become? Would he savor this moment of revenge on his brothers? Would Joseph withhold the desperately needed grain to pay them back for their blatant cruelty when he was just a teenager? A man who lacked character would have reveled in this moment of domination, triumph and prosperity. But listen to what happened when Joseph revealed his true identity to his brothers: "He threw his arms around his brother Benjamin and wept, and Benjamin embraced him, weeping. And he kissed all his brothers and wept over them" (45:14-15).

The only ornery comment he made during the entire reunion was, "Don't quarrel on the way!" (45:24). (As the youngest of five boys in my family, I must confess that I can relate to that shrewd jab!)

Joseph proved beyond a shadow of a doubt that he was a leader with true character. When no one else was looking, he refused to sleep with Potiphar's wife. When his brothers failed to recognize him, he revealed himself to them and forgave them for their wicked betrayal many years earlier. Joseph could have continued to conceal his identity and reject their cry for help. But this godly man displayed his beneficent character when it counted most.

Joseph discovered, too, that morality is its own reward. He had suffered unjustly for his dreams at the hands of his brothers. He was imprisoned for a sexual assault that never took place. But in the end, Joseph understood the joy and fulfillment that results from a life devoted to the development of character. In the words of the poem quoted by Dr. Laura at the beginning of this chapter:

> I know what others may never know,
> I can never fool myself and so . . .
> Whatever happens I want to be,
> Self-respecting & conscience free!

"Thoroughly living life requires initiative, risk-taking, sustained action against odds, sacrificing for ideals and for others, leaps of faith."
—Dr. Laura[1]

What Broth Is to Soup

"COURAGE IS TO LIFE what broth is to soup. It is the very context that gives experiences, events, and opportunities a special richness, flavor, and meaning."[2]

Dr. Laura is constantly urging her callers to practice courage as they face the struggles and challenges of day-to-day life. She herself has had to summon up courage on several fronts because of the strong stands she has taken both on her radio program and in her writing. Here are just a few of her attacks on popular positions in our culture: 1) *Working moms.* She insists that couples can find a way to ensure that at least one parent is home for the children who are not yet in school (See chapter 10.); 2) *Premarital sex.* Dr. Laura is uncompromising on her commitment to sexual relationships being reserved for the marriage commitment (See chapter 17.); 3) *Abortion.* She unswervingly believes that human life begins at conception, and that adoption is the best solution to an "unwanted pregnancy." (See chapter 11.)

Dr. Schlessinger's dauntless commitment to these positions has not exactly endeared her to some very vocal groups in North America! Many families are trying to "have it all" with both parents working full-time in order to pay for better clothes, newer cars, bigger homes and, of course, day care. Singles want to be free to have sex with anyone and everyone they date without being concerned about consequences or obligations. This has led to the murderous act of abortion in an attempt to relieve both partners of their solemn responsibility to the human life they created together.

Obviously, Dr. Laura is stepping on some sensitive toes in these three areas. She is to be applauded for her gallant, consistent position with regard to parents being with their young children during the formative years. Those who embrace biblical standards should be thankful for her daring confrontation of sex outside of marriage. We should laud her support for the sanctity of human life at conception. This is courage. Such courage, she points out, is the proving ground for our value system: "Courage is also what gives values vibrancy. So many people espouse values about sex, abortion, honesty, etc., until the dilemma is theirs. Then, because of their particular circumstances, selfish needs, and uncomfortable feelings, the values become optional."[3]

Chapter 3 of her book *How Could You Do That?!* is entitled "I Know It's Right . . . But. . . ." Dr. Laura devotes this chapter to the harsh realities people face when they are challenged to act boldly, when they are forced to determine what really matters. Here are some examples of the escape routes that are often chosen:

> "But . . . I'd rather be the victim."
> "But . . . I did the right thing and I'm still miserable."
> "But . . . I'm not really selling out, am I?"
> "But . . . it's not what I planned."
> "But . . . it's not convenient."
> "But . . . it's not fair."
> "But . . . the other guys will think I'm a wuss."[4]

Dr. Laura then proceeds to examine each of these supposed justifications for taking the easy way out. With the use of powerful illustrations from her talk show, she urges the reader to choose a courageous approach to the obstacles of life.

Choosing Victimhood

A man named Pete was married to a husband-beater. At thirty-one, his forty-year-old wife abused alcohol, cocaine and other assorted drugs. Rehab? She'd been there, done that. She refused to bother with it ever again.

Pete told Dr. Laura that he had a hard time dealing with her addictions. Though he believed in keeping his marriage vows, he wondered if he should stay in the relationship. Pete had played the martyr before, but this was ridiculous. Marriage at all costs?

When Dr. Laura began to give him an out, Pete became reluctant. Was this man really worried about keeping his vows or was he afraid that if he left her he would become a martyr without a cause? Pete had to agree that he somewhat relished his victim status. He gained attention by playing the victim. He didn't want to be responsible for the choices in his life.

Dr. Laura went on to point out that Pete and his wife were actually very similar. Neither wanted to face self or the world. She used drugs. He used his suffering over his plight of living with an addict. Add to this the fact that Pete's loyalty was foolish because it supported the illegal activities of a wife who absolutely refused to change. The doctor urged Pete to step up to the plate and do the courageous thing: leave his wife and get some help for some of his own problems.

Les Miserables

Dr. Laura talks about another common error in our thinking that keeps us from acting with courage. Sometimes when we do the right thing, we still feel miserable! Life does not always reward us instantly with the happiness and success that we think might accompany ethical behavior.

Elizabeth left an abusive husband two-and-a-half years ago. She wrote to Dr. Schlessinger to complain that she now found herself increasingly tired and depressed as she worked to support herself and the two children. Why wasn't she happy all the time after doing the right thing?

Dr. Laura tried to point out to Elizabeth that her life was indeed much better than it had been with a man who physically and emotionally trashed her and her children. She was now focusing on some other tough aspects of being a single mother without fully appreciating her new freedom from an evil, domineering man. No doubt, in the future, Elizabeth would be able to experience more and more happiness. Her courage would ultimately be rewarded.

Selling Out

Dr. Schlessinger relates the story of Linda who admitted that she was tolerating unethical things at her present job so that she could get on to something bigger and better herself. Even though she had witnessed racial discrimination of coworkers in a major department store, Linda was afraid to blow the whistle for fear of her own job security.

After talking with Dr. Laura, Linda decided to do the right thing, the courageous thing. She told her supervisor and the personnel manager that she simply would not sell out and look the other way when inappropriate behavior or injustices were displayed by her and the other executives. Linda eventually lost that job, but she had no regrets. Her courage was rewarded with a clear conscience.

A Change of Plans

Michael, at twenty years of age, was confronting the prospect of doing right after being wronged. He had been having a sexual relationship with a woman who was using birth control pills. She intentionally went off the pill and became pregnant. Michael complained that he had been emotionally blackmailed.

Dr. Laura clarified this simple fact: The child does not care about the shenanigans—he just wants a daddy! Michael was responsible to be this child's father and to behave in a decent manner around the child's mother even though they wouldn't be living together under the same roof. "It's not what I planned" does not give anyone an excuse to act in a cowardly, irresponsible way.

Inconvenience

Acting with courage is often not convenient! In the above story of Michael, it is not a favorable circumstance for either mom or dad. They will eventually have their own spouses and children, and the prospect of having to work out visitation times and schedules is not a pleasant one. But for the sake of this child for whom both of them are responsible, it is a bold adventure upon which they must embark.

It's Not Fair

Fifty-year-old Brenda was disgusted when she called 1-800-DRLAURA. Her husband was a military man who had sent his elderly mother money for eighteen years. His nine brothers and sisters lived in close proximity to their mother, but it was Brenda's husband who helped her the most. It just didn't seem fair.

Dr. Laura pointed out the backward reasoning that Brenda had embraced in her bitter reaction to her husband's benevolence. She should have rejoiced about being married to the one out of ten children who was an ethical person! Instead, Brenda was faulting him for doing the right thing even though his brothers and sisters were not honoring their mother.

According to Dr. Schlessinger, it takes special courage to obey one's conscience while others disregard the basic moral and ethical principles that produce decent behavior.

Called a Wuss

Thirty-one-year-old Mark knew he was doing the right thing by being a stay-at-home dad, but he struggled with being considered a wuss by other guys his age who dutifully go to work each day. Dr. Laura came long with some timely reminders for Mark.

Life is a series of choices. Driving to a corner, one must pick a direction and proceed. In that selection, something will be missed. By turning right, you miss out on whatever is to the left. To get anywhere, we must leave something else behind.

Mark had chosen to be there for his son. In this scenario, his wife had a better job with full benefits. It made sense for him to elect the stay-at-home status and find part-time work he could do out of the house. Rather than be apologetic for this decision, Mark should be proud! But it took courage to stay the course when his friends implied that he was a sissy for staying home.

Be of Good Courage

The Scripture, too, calls us to bravely tackle life in all of its complexities. The challenge to "be of good courage" occurs nineteen times from Numbers to Isaiah. Paul twice told the men in the middle of a life-threatening hurricane to "keep up your courage" (Acts 27:22, 25).

Jesus indicated that following Him will mean that we must "[e]nter through the narrow gate. For wide is the gate and broad is the road that leads to destruction, and many enter through it. But small is the gate and narrow the road that leads to life, and only a few find it" (Matthew 7:13-14). (The word "narrow" could be translated "difficult.")

One artist captured the sentiment of this passage by painting two pathways. One road started wide and finished extremely narrow. The other pathway began as a cramped crevice which was difficult to enter but became a broad expanse toward the end. This is, in many ways, an accurate depiction.

Let's face it: Choosing the easy way is easier! All of us naturally lean in that direction. We need the Scripture and people like Dr. Laura to remind us that we can bravely face the formidable tasks and responsibilities before us, and "be of good courage."

"If I am not for myself, who will be? But if I am only for myself, who am I?"
—Jewish Proverb[1]

Where's Your Conscience?

"YOU HAVE CONSCIENCE," SAYS Dr. Laura in the introduction to her book *How Could You Do That?!,* "when you most often compel yourself to do what is right for its own sake."[2] Then, at the beginning of chapter 2, she quotes President Abraham Lincoln: "It is the eternal struggle between these two principles—right and wrong—throughout the world. They are the two principles that have stood face to face from the beginning of time; and will ever continue to struggle."[3]

Dr. Schlessinger defines conscience as "our capacity to judge ourselves in moral terms and to conform to those standards and values that we make a part of our inner being."[4]

All of us have been born with this instinctive knowledge of right and wrong, Dr. Laura insists. She sees the human conscience playing a role both in creating negatives to be avoided and positives to be attained. This sense of good and evil will push us to avoid the two painful emotions triggered by doing the wrong thing: ". . . guilt (internal pain from the disappointment in self) and shame (public awareness of our transgressions with the threat of condemnation and punishment). . . ."[5]

Our conscience will also remind us of the good feelings which result from doing the right thing, such as "pride (in our fulfillment of goodness), compassion, empathy, love, and identification (seeing ourselves in others, thereby imagining how our actions would feel if directed onto us)."[6]

Dr. Schlessinger also points out the two stages of conscience and their respective origins: "In childhood, conscience is our internalized fear of losing our parents' love and support. In adulthood, it's something we impose upon ourselves in order to become complete human beings."[7]

Knowing the difference between right and wrong forces us to make choices—and sets us apart from lower animals: "We have responsibility because we have control. The metaphorical point of Adam and Eve leaving the Garden of Eden is that humans have the ability and the inescapable requirement of making choices."[8]

Then Dr. Laura gets right to the point by demonstrating in extremely practical terms how this affects our everyday lives: "These decisions are made continuously: from parking in handicapped spaces to save yourself time and steps, to justifying your lack of quantity time with your children and family by exalting quality time."[9]

This is so pragmatic it hurts. Dr. Schlessinger digs right into the heart of everyday decisions which often must be calculated within seconds. Most of us have contemplated parking in that handicapped spot with the rationalization that "there just can't be that many disabled people!" Have we not assuaged our conscience with the notion that we are spending "quality time" with our spouse or children because of other sacrifices we are not willing to make?

This is the blessing and the curse of having this inner voice. But the conscience can only announce the choice. We must choose. And that decision will impact our lives for days, weeks, months—maybe even years—into the future.

The Whole Truth, and Nothing but the Truth

Another matter of conscience is truth-telling. Dr. Laura clearly states that "white lies are wrong."[10] A twenty-two-year-old woman was dating a guy whom she considered to be the man she wanted to marry. But a year and a half before they met, she had filed for chapter 7 bankruptcy. Now she was afraid to tell her boyfriend. Though he knew that her credit was not good and that she had debts to pay off, she was fearful that a complete revelation of her circumstances would lead to a breakup. She wrote for advice on how far to go in telling the truth. Dr. Laura replied with this: "I never believe that people who keep their weaknesses and faults secret have any real intent of changing. They are too busy trying to look better so that they can get what they want. This is an issue of character, not money."[11]

But when pressed on the issue of sharing the whole truth in every situation, Dr. Laura is sometimes evasive. For instance, she embraces a "don't ask, don't tell" philosophy—if someone doesn't ask, you don't have to tell! She often advises people against telling the full story about past sins if the confession would not ultimately help the person being told. *U.S.News & World Report,* in a cover story on Dr. Laura, said: "Schlessinger admits now and then that moral absolutes don't always hold. More than once she has advised callers against honesty, which 'can be evil if it's harmful or cruel.' "[12]

On June 1, 1998, a father called Dr. Laura's show to ask a question about just how much he should tell his children about the past. The dad said he didn't want to lie to the kids. Dr. Laura asked this loaded, point-blank question: "So you think it is always wrong to lie?" He fumbled around for an answer while she reloaded. Then she said, "A lie may sometimes be good if it prevents a greater evil."[13]

She used three intriguing illustrations to back up her position. First, Bill is chasing Joe with a gun. Joe evades him by ducking into an alley near where you are standing. Bill asks you which way Joe was running. If you tell the truth, Joe may be killed. Second, a mass murderer runs out of bullets and asks you where he can find some more. Do you tell him where to find more ammunition and risk more people being shot? Or do you lie about it to stall the mass murderer?

And third, a parent is asked by his child if he experimented with drugs when he was a teen. Should the parent answer at all? Dr. Schlessinger would say that the parent has no such obligation because it places the parent and teen on the same level. Then the parent becomes a "buddy" instead of an authority figure. Respect for the parent is a higher principle than telling the truth about the past, according to the doctor.

Granted, the first two illustrations are extreme. Dr. Laura did not discuss other possible responses in those scenarios.

Let's look at another scenario. A young man was looking for a compact disc at a friend's house. Quite accidentally, he found pornographic materials that were "somewhat hidden" under shelves in the room. Fearing for the exposure of a young boy who lived in that house to these indecent materials, he called Dr. Laura to ask her if he should confront the man of the house with his discovery. Talk radio's leading lady told him plainly that it was "none of his business" and that he shouldn't go "poking around."[14]

In my opinion, and in the light of Scripture as I understand it, that was not the best advice. This man should have been confronted because the pornography did pose a risk for others who may have found it. Also, there is a good chance that the wife was not aware of the presence of this sexually explicit material in her home. Does she not deserve to know about her husband's habit?

Balancing Encouragement and Confession

These can often be difficult issues with which to grapple. The Bible seems to balance two realities—telling the whole truth while being sensitive to the need to say that which helps someone and the need to confess sin that directly affects someone else. Consider these Scripture verses: "[S]peaking the truth in love . . . each of you must put off falsehood and speak truthfully to his neighbor" (Ephesians 4:15, 25). "Confess your sins to each other" (James 5:16). "Do not let any unwholesome talk come out of your mouths, but only what is helpful for building others up . . ." (Ephesians 4:29).

A woman who had adopted a girl called *The Dr. Laura Show*. The child had been conceived through a violent rape. The adoptive mother wanted to know if there would ever be any circumstances under which she should tell this girl the truth about her conception. Dr. Laura said she should never share that story. This advice lines up with Ephesians 4:29 quoted above. In no way would this "build up" that child. It would be devastating news with nothing but negative consequences.

Now consider another scenario. On June 24, 1998, a woman called Dr. Laura to confess that, after many years of faithfulness to her husband, she had recently committed adultery with an old acquaintance while at a convention in another town. The lady was quite remorseful and very determined that she would never do it again. But the nagging question remained: "Should I confess this to my husband?"

Dr. Schlessinger told her that it would be "selfish" to place that burden on her husband. Her punishment would be adequate enough—living for the rest of her life with the painful memory of her moral failure. Her sense of guilt was good in that it demonstrated she was not a "creep," Dr. Laura said. She concluded by saying that this would be a good time for the woman to pray.

Though this was a noble recommendation, it did not offer the redemptive lift this woman so desperately needed. The Bible would instruct this lady to confess her sin to the Lord first and secure His forgiveness (1 John 1:9). Then she should seek her husband's forgiveness for her immoral act as given in James 5:16: "Confess your sins to each other." In doing this, she could secure a clear conscience with both God and husband. Her heart would be clean (healed), and her guilt would be vanquished. Would there be repercussions with her husband? Most likely. Would there be difficult memories with which to cope? Certainly. But she would know the freedom of forgiveness. We must obey God's Word and allow the Lord to handle the outcome.

To summarize, the Bible indicates that we should confess private sins (whether of mind or body) privately—to God, and personal sin personally—to the one who has been impacted by our sinful act. And we are wise to confess public sin publicly. When our iniquity has affected a group, we should stand before them all to ask forgiveness. We are to tell the truth. We are to do so lovingly. And we are to keep in mind the importance of building others up by what we say.

Truth and Consequences

Discipleship Journal had an interesting article entitled "Is It Ever Right to Do Wrong?" Authors Mark Fackler and Christopher Bunn point out that sometimes perfect honesty appears to result in unpleasant consequences. But those who choose strict obedience to God's commands trust the Creator to handle the outcome. By way of illustration, they include a humorous and profound story from Corrie Ten Boom's book *The Hiding Place:*

> Corrie's sister was determined not to lie, even to the
> Nazis. When soldiers came to the door, looking for

healthy young men to work in their munitions factories, she told them the truth.

"Where are your men?" the soldiers demanded.

"Under the table," she replied.

Her nephews were, in fact, under the table—in an underground room. The trap door that led to it was under the kitchen table, hidden by a rug. The Nazis glanced under the table, concluded the woman was crazy, and left.[15]

One could argue that Corrie's sister was hoping that the soldiers would indeed think she was demented in saying that her nephews were "under the table." It may even appear that she used a form of deception. But there is no reason to assume that she put her hope in the Nazi's consternation. Knowing the godly nature of the people involved, it is clear that they put their hope in the Lord. These women purposed to tell the truth and let God take care of the repercussions. And on this occasion the reward for their dangerous honesty was protection.

However, not everyone who tells the whole truth in situations like this will be shielded from harm. Foxe's Book of Martyrs is filled with story after story of those who died in an excruciating manner for their unabashed honesty. Their ultimate compensation will come someday when Christ returns to take them to their eternal reward in heaven.

Telling the truth may sometimes result in a jail term. Those we love may be hurt by deep, dark secrets that are revealed. The pathway of honesty may lead to insecurity in relationships. The parent who truthfully answers the question about drug use in the past may experience a temporary lack of respect from his or her children. But ultimately, God will honor that kind of humility and honesty. Those children will someday admire the courage it took to tell them the truth.

The Bible is very straightforward on this issue: Speak truthfully and let God handle the outcome.

In this particular conscience-related matter, Dr. Laura does not seem to fully measure up to the letter of God's law. She allows for too much flexibility with the clear instruction to tell the "whole truth."

The Biblical Parallels

However, Dr. Schlessinger does suggest many principles through both her writing and her radio advice that parallel the teachings of the testaments with regard to the human conscience. We are indeed born with a conscience—a moral capacity to comprehend the distinction between right and wrong. Adam and Eve immediately sensed the need to clothe themselves and hide from God when they sinned. Why? Because the guilt of their sin produced their initial realization of shame. They had violated the moral law of the Creator, and they felt pain in their hearts because of it.

Dr. Laura asks us to consider how we would feel if what we did to others was directed back to us. This is reminiscent of our Lord's challenge in Luke 6:31: "Do to others as you would have them do to you."

Many of the troubled callers who ask Dr. Laura for advice are trying to cope with people in their lives who have abused them and thereby blunted their consciences. In the words of Isaiah the prophet, they "call evil good and good evil" (Isaiah 5:20). Not only do these folks reap what they have sown for themselves, but many others are impacted by their sinful choices.

A woman calls about her boyfriend who has gotten her pregnant even though he already has three other children by as many women.

A tearful husband relates the story of his flirtatious wife who has recently confessed to having affairs with several men.

The Bible refers to such consciences as having been "seared as with a hot iron" (1 Timothy 4:2). This is very descriptive. It is the picture of nerve endings that have been cauterized and thus desensitized. Such a thing can happen to any person who persists in the perpetual violation of the conscience. This is the only possible explanation for the horrors inflicted by those who murdered millions of Jews during the Holocaust.

So Dr. Schlessinger talks a lot about the wonderful benefits of maintaining a clear conscience. She places a high value on sincere apologies and "making things right." A woman wrote to Dr. Laura about her wild overreaction to her teen daughter's behavior. The woman was afraid she would "lose authority" if she apologized. Dr. Laura gave this advice:

> You must apologize for getting carried away with your anger. . . . She will not lose respect for your honesty, nor will you lose status as authority. . . . With this apology and promise you model behavior for her with you and everyone else in her life.[16]

There are also the four "R's" of repentance according to Dr. Laura:

- Responsibility—recognize we've done wrong.
- Regret—have true remorse for the wrong and the resultant pain and problems.
- Resolve—be committed never to repeat the act regardless of the temptation or situation.
- Repair—do what we can to apologize directly to the injured party.[17]

Paul the apostle announces the key to a happy, healthy relationship with God and other people: "I strive always to keep my conscience clear before God and man" (Acts 24:16). He was able to look straight at the members of the Sanhedrin and say, "I have fulfilled my duty to God in all good conscience to this day" (23:1).

The spiritual revival that began at the Ebenezer Baptist Church in Saskatoon, Saskatchewan, Canada, in the fall of 1971 gained its impetus by the bold proclamation that the church (meaning its people) must return to the utterly simple principle of a clear conscience "before God and man." Hundreds of thousands of lives have been transformed wherever this message has been preached and acted upon.

In many ways, Dr. Laura Schlessinger is, via radio, a daily, international reminder of these two vital and scriptural truths: First, God has given us the ability to know right from wrong; second, we will be blessed when we do the right thing.

"That moment of physical pleasure
will now dictate the rest of my life."
—Hal, a caller

Delayed Gratification

"HUMANS ARE THE ONLY creatures on earth who take pleasure in resisting temptation, easy and fast gratification, and constant pleasure seeking. We respect, admire, trust, and love those whose struggle between self-interest and commitment tilts toward the latter: commitment, honor, duty, compassion."[1]

In this paragraph from *How Could You Do That?!*, Dr. Laura addresses one of the most despised phrases in our language today: delayed gratification. This concept is about as welcome as a pulled hamstring muscle would be to Michael Jordan at the beginning of the NBA playoffs. It is true that there is a certain pleasure to be experienced by those who are willing to wait. And we do respect those who choose commitment and honor over self-interest. But when faced with the challenge to postpone the satisfaction of our own desires, we must each confess to the intense struggle that ensues.

When we lose, there will be repercussions. "We do wrong because in our inner battle morality is lost to immediate self-interest. And the reward for that is a moment's thrill and a potpourri of destructive consequences."[2]

We've Got Tonight—Who Needs Tomorrow?

We don't have to live a long time to understand the severe consequences of acting on our impulses and giving in to the moment. Dr. Laura shares this story from a caller named Danielle. Married less than three years, she had already given birth to a child and conducted a four-month affair. Why? There were pressures, responsibilities and financial problems. That sounded a lot like real-life for most people. Danielle agreed: "Yeah, I guess so, and now he's left me and I want to stay."[3]

In her incisive way, Dr. Schlessinger zeroes in on Danielle's dilemma: She picked her right to happiness over her commitments and obligations to her husband and son. Danielle was foolish to think that those real-life burdens affected only her. She incorrectly assumed that the problems she faced could be cured with illicit sex. Ultimately, her husband decided that she was not the kind of person he wanted to be married to when times get tough. Danielle had some moments of pleasure with her toy boy. But now she must face the long-term implications of divorce, separation from her son and a host of other complications.

Consider Hal's plight. Only twenty-one, he admitted to Dr. Laura that he professed love for his girlfriend because that would make her happy, and he would be rewarded with sexual intercourse. But this led to pregnancy. And she insists on keeping the baby. Now what? Hal had a revelation: "I'm suddenly smacked in the face with the awareness of how that moment of physical pleasure will now dictate the rest of my life."[4]

In a powerful statement concerning the vital distinction between pleasure and happiness, Dr. Laura compares pleasure to a discreet and enjoyable experience—like a sugar-covered donut, listening to music, a foot rub or watching an absorbing movie. But the catch is that this great feeling is transitory and often quite superficial: "In this regard, pleasure is an event;

happiness is a process. Pleasure is an end point; happiness is the journey. Pleasure is material; happiness is spiritual. Pleasure is self-involved; happiness is outer—and other—involved."[5]

Dr. Schlessinger is quick to remind us of the frustrating time factor inherent in any given moment of pleasure: "This very moment, any moment, lasts but a moment."[6] However, we may live with the memory and the consequences of those few and fleeting seconds for a lifetime. This is the transitory nature of pleasure: "A deep happiness rarely comes from immediately pleasurable behaviors and experiences. Pleasure is time-limited to the pleasurable input."[7]

Avoiding Pain

Dr. Laura contends that giving in to "the moment" is often the way we choose to avoid some kind of pain or discomfort. A caller named Mike had a repetitive behavior which he couldn't seem to stop. When he acted on this impulse, he felt better—but only temporarily. That was the catch. Just like a drug addict, Mike was willing to do whatever it took to feel better right now. The good doctor offered this challenging question: "How can you ever get better unless you're willing to tolerate that pain? Which means when the need comes you tolerate not feeling good right now. I need you to suffer, Babe."[8]

Dr. Laura tells about the replacement that must be made if we are to become mature: "This is the fundamental exchange: immediate comfort or gratification versus ideals that transcend comfort and build character."[9]

These are challenging concepts. Do we want to live our lives for the moment, or will we choose to make decisions based on the long haul? Dr. Laura reveals a "trick" she uses in this regard to get callers focused on the big picture of their lives: "I ask them to project themselves into what they'd like their future to be and then to ask themselves if this decision will help lead them there."[10]

Moses: Looking Ahead

Once again, Dr. Schlessinger has highlighted a vital biblical principle. Delayed gratification is as old as the temptation of the first humans in the Garden of Eden. Things would be quite different if Adam and Eve had been able to obey God's command to stay away from the tree of the knowledge of good and evil. In His time, the Creator would have explained everything they needed to know about that unique tree. But Eve, allowing herself to be seduced by the serpent, made a hasty decision to taste that fruit now! Adam, standing nearby, decided to eat some, too. Their decisions led to a lifetime of sorrow and suffering for both.

In Moses, however, we see a man who cared more about the big picture than mere momentary delights. The book of Hebrews offers this historical perspective on his life:

> By faith Moses, when he had grown up, refused to be known as the son of Pharaoh's daughter. He chose to be mistreated along with the people of God rather than to enjoy the pleasures of sin for a short time. He regarded disgrace for the sake of Christ as of greater value than the treasures of Egypt, because he was looking ahead to his reward. By faith he left Egypt, not fearing the king's anger; he persevered because he saw him who is invisible. (Hebrews 11:24-27)

In both Dr. Laura's material and the Bible we see this acknowledgment: There is pleasure in sin! This cannot be denied. The person who breaks the rules and defies God's moral law will experience a thrill. However, it is the quality and duration

of that excitement that is in question. God's Word declares
that the pleasure of sin lasts only "a short time" (11:25).

Solomon struggled with this reality throughout the book of
Ecclesiastes. One day he decided to walk away from God and
experience "life under the sun"—that is, a life of pretending
that there was no one above the sun. Ecclesiastes is the original
Humanist Manifesto. Solomon experimented with everything
conceivable in a vain attempt to fill the God-shaped vacuum of
his soul. Lots of wine to drink. Unlimited women for sexual fa-
vors—700 wives, 300 concubines! (1 Kings 11:3). Intense
work projects to keep him busy. Wealth galore.

But nothing could satisfy his desperate sense of emptiness.
He admits:

> I denied myself nothing my eyes desired;
>   I refused my heart no pleasure.
> My heart took delight in all my work,
>   and this was the reward for all my labor.
> Yet when I surveyed all that my hands had done
>   and what I toiled to achieve,
> everything was meaningless, a chasing after the wind;
>   nothing was gained under the sun.
> (Ecclesiastes 2:10-11)

The king plunged into the world of instant gratification and
found it utterly lacking in its ability to satisfy beyond that instant.
It was short-term titillation followed by long-term disappointment. Solomon had all of the wealth and power required to pursue
hedonism with a vengeance. But when he did, he was devastated
to find out just how fleeting it all could be.

Moses, on the other hand, accepted the ephemeral quality of
sinful pleasure as fact. With this understanding, he decided to live
his life while "looking ahead to his reward . . . because he saw him

who is invisible" (Hebrews 11:26-27). This great man of God was willing to suffer delayed gratification for the eternal gratification of a clear conscience and being in the kingdom of God forever.

This principle weaves its way through both the Old and New Testaments. We are called to deny ourselves certain things we may be tempted to go after here so that we will experience everlasting joy hereafter. Paul puts it this way:

> I consider that our present sufferings are not worth comparing with the glory that will be revealed in us. . . . For our light and momentary troubles are achieving for us an eternal glory that far outweighs them all. So we fix our eyes not on what is seen, but on what is unseen. For what is seen is temporary, but what is unseen is eternal. (Romans 8:18; 2 Corinthians 4:17-18)

Does this mean that those who want to live by the Good Book will not experience any physical or earthly pleasures at all? No! There are legitimate, God-honoring forms of exhilaration. And these become even more special and enjoyable for those who put them in their proper place. But we get caught in the trap of instant gratification and its long-term consequences when we place too much emphasis on those feelings and experiences that are temporal.

Thanks, Dr. Laura!

We can be grateful for Dr. Schlessinger's emphasis on the character-building quality of delayed gratification. In a culture that is obsessed with instant everything, Dr. Laura has faithfully proclaimed this simple (and biblical) truth: Some things are worth waiting for!

Thanks, Doctor.

Issues of the Id

[1] id \'id\ n: the undifferentiated source of the organism's energy from which both ego and libido are derived.

—from *Webster's Seventh New Collegiate Dictionary*

Dr. Laura Schlessinger has some interesting things to say about self- esteem and self-reliance—issues of the "id," or "self." We will explore these here in Part 3.

*"Self-esteem is always
forged from your efforts."*
—Dr. Laura

8

New Attitude

THOSE WHO ARE FAMILIAR with The Dr. Laura Show get used to hearing her theme song: "Oo-oo, Oo-oo-oo, I've got new attitude!" Dr. Laura explains why she chose this upbeat number: "I begin each hour of my program with 'I've Got a New Attitude,' sung by Patti LaBelle, because it expresses my belief that it is attitude, infinitely more than circumstance, that determines the quality of life."[1]

Obtaining Self-esteem

In her book *Ten Stupid Things Women Do to Mess Up Their Lives,* Dr. Schlessinger talks a lot about the importance of self-esteem in order to obtain that new attitude. How one gets and enhances self-esteem is where Dr. Laura differs from many other psychologists.

Dr. Chris Mruk, an associate professor of psychology at Firelands College of Bowling Green State University, defines self-esteem as: "The lived status of one's individual competence and personal worthiness at dealing with the challenges of life over time."[2]

In his book, *Self-Esteem: Research, Theory, and Practice,* Dr. Mruk concludes with a chapter entitled "Enhancing Self-Esteem Phenomenologic-ally." In excruciatingly careful detail, he describes psychoeducational group therapy designed for eight to fifteen people. There are a series of five to six two-hour meetings over one-and-a-half months. It is all very technical, very involved. But is it necessary?

Dr. Laura Schlessinger would say "no." There is a much more direct route to self-esteem which costs a lot less than six weeks with a shrink. She asks the apropos question to get at the heart of the issue:

> Chicken or the egg? Do you have to have self-esteem before or after you behave with honor and courage? Popular psychology says self-esteem comes first. So my next question becomes, "Then where the heck do you get the self-esteem?"[3]

She agrees with the answer to that question given by Dr. Harold W. Stevenson when he says:

> Self-esteem theorists have it backward. Meaningful self-evaluation and positive self-esteem are usually results, not antecedents, of accomplishment. Praise is only one source of feedback; self-esteem more often comes from an awareness that the requirements of a sought-after goal have been mastered. . . . Feeling good is fine; it is even better when we have something to feel good about.[4]

Dr. Laura summarizes by saying: "Self-esteem is always forged from your efforts."[5]

My father used to say, "God can't steer a parked car." He was a great advocate of getting out there and doing something rather than just passively sitting back to watch. Dr. Schlessinger concurs: "It is the process of doing, of committing yourself to something that makes the difference in your enjoyment of life and your satisfaction with self."[6]

She gave this advice to one caller who wanted to feel better about herself: "Go make yourself feel like you have purpose on this earth. Go feel like your existence makes the world different. Go do something that gives your life meaning."[7]

Dr. Laura, then, is committed to the principle that positive self-esteem must be derived from our performance. She refers to self-worth as "the gift you have to earn."[8] It is forged by handling the difficulties of life with our best efforts and unwavering tenacity: "Accomplishment, leading to self-esteem, is not just about doing something. . . . It is about the courage to persist through pain and failure and self-doubt; to go past splat . . . to focus on self-effort as the avenue to self-esteem and positive identity."[9]

Acceptance of oneself is then predicated on our response to difficulties that arise as we attempt to "do life": "The quality of our lives ultimately depends upon the courage we extend to deal with hurt and risk in a creative way: That is the road to ever growing self-esteem."[10]

The Source of Self-esteem

Self-esteem must ultimately come from deep within each of us, according to Dr. Schlessinger. She says we achieve a sense of worthiness by believing in a universal inalienable right to respect, honor, commitment, caring and love. Then we earn it by our courageous efforts in all areas of life. With religious conviction, she declares: "Self-esteem is earned. Amen."[11]

Listening and Doing

There is a sense in which Scripture would support the assertion that "self-esteem is earned." A clear connection can be made between the way we obey God's Word and the way we feel about ourselves. Jesus said: "Blessed rather are those who hear the word of God and obey it" (Luke 11:28), and "Now that you know these things, you will be blessed [happy] if you do them" (John 13:17).

James echoes the same truth:

> Do not merely listen to the word, and so deceive yourselves. Do what it says. . . . [T]he man who looks intently into the perfect law that gives freedom, and continues to do this, not forgetting what he has heard, but doing it—he will be blessed in what he does. (James 1:22, 25).

Joy, fulfillment and an overall sense of well-being will preside in our lives when we have followed the Lord's will. The opposite is true too. Disobedience will obviously lead us to a struggle with guilt and shame which will attack our sense of self-esteem. We will not "feel good about ourselves." The psalmist expressed it this way:

> When I kept silent,
>   my bones wasted away
>   through my groaning all day long.
> For day and night
>   your hand was heavy upon me;
> my strength was sapped
>   as in the heat of summer. *Selah*
> Then I acknowledged my sin to you
>   and did not cover up my iniquity.

> I said, "I will confess
>> my transgressions to the LORD"—
> and you forgave
>> the guilt of my sin. *Selah*
> (Psalm 32:3-5)

David reminds us that in our attempt to cover up our sin when we have failed God, we will lose the joy and blessedness of our relationship with Him. But thankfully, all of that can be quickly restored through genuine repentance. As we acknowledge the transgression, we can be forgiven. The guilt is removed. Self-esteem returns.

There is a profound simplicity in this emphasis by both Dr. Laura and the Bible: "Do the right thing and you will feel right about yourself. Do the wrong thing, and you will feel lousy about yourself." I can think of some angry letters I have written which should not have been sent, some stupid statements I've made that should not have been verbalized. But because those letters were mailed and those words were uttered, I suffered the consequences for those actions. And it was not good for my self-esteem!

Fearfully and Wonderfully Made, but Fallen

There is, however, a subtle but vital distinction that should be made between Dr. Schlessinger's view on self-esteem and what we find in Scripture. She would say that the true source of self-esteem is found within each of us. We are all given a certain potential when we are born, and we can shape our self-image positively or negatively according to our choices and behavior. Dr. Laura firmly believes that we are "fearfully and wonderfully made" (Psalm 139:14) in God's image. But she is less clear on the fallen condition of human beings. (See chapter 18.)

Because of the fact that "all have sinned and fall short of the glory of God" (Romans 3:23), we experience guilt and shame on a regular basis. Low self-esteem is thus generated by our degenerate thoughts and actions. Apart from the forgiveness and cleansing that Christ alone can offer, we have no right to feel good about ourselves. We desperately need to be restored to His image.

So, the preeminent basis for self-esteem is simply this: God loves us! In fact, He considered us to be of so much value that He was willing to sacrifice His only Son on our behalf. How much are we worth to the Creator? We are worth the death of Jesus Christ! This is truly beyond our most profound comprehension.

Charles Wesley attempted to put this spectacular reality into a hymn:

> He left His Father's throne above,
> So free, so infinite His grace;
> Emptied Himself of all but love,
> And bled for Adam's helpless race.
> 'Tis mercy all, immense and free!
> For, O my God, it found out me.
>
> Amazing love! How can it be
> That Thou, my God, shouldst die for me![12]

When we become the children of God through repentance and faith in Christ, we are members of a family in which self-esteem is built not around good works that we perform for God. Rather, it is based upon the singular good work performed by God when He sent His Son to die for our sins. Now we revel in the righteousness of Christ which has become our own: "God made him who had no sin to be sin for us, so that in him we might become the righteousness of God" (2 Corinthians 5:21).

Our self-esteem will grow in proportion to our submission to His will and His commands. We will feel good about ourselves in the sense that we are reaping the benefits of obeying God. And within our hearts we will know that it is the Lord Jesus who gives us the strength to choose His way.

Dr. Laura is right in saying that people who focus on "doing the right thing" will build positive self-esteem. It is possible to achieve a certain level of respectability in our character through self-righteousness, but God declares that this kind of piety is ultimately as worthless as "filthy rags" (Isaiah 64:6). The apostle Paul clarifies the origins of his own righteousness: "That I may gain Christ and be found in him, not having a righteousness of my own that comes from the law, but that which is through faith in Christ—the righteousness that comes from God and is by faith" (Philippians 3:8-9).

Apart from the gospel, all of our attempts to develop an honorable self-image will be frustrated by our inability to deal with the core issue—we are sinners and we need a Savior!

This is the critical distinction with the issue of self-esteem. Dr. Laura indicates that a positive self-image can be obtained through choosing right over wrong and good over evil. She implies that righteousness can be attained through human aspiration:

> Having the power to choose between good and evil is what makes human beings truly free. Our freedom consists of mastery over oneself, over our whims, temptations, immediate gratification, self-centeredness, and greed, etc. That freedom to choose challenges us all the time.[13]

Such a humanistic approach to holiness caresses the ego because we can take the credit for choosing good over evil, mastering our passions and creating our own righteousness.

Scripture, on the other hand, indicates that in our fallen condition, we have lost the power to select right over wrong. Our natural bent is in the direction of evil. It is logical that as sinners we should lack self-esteem. We need a whole new heart.

Self-esteem built on this foundation will give our lives lasting joy and deep meaning.

"If she is successful, it may be in part because she offers something pills and feel-good therapies don't: the notion that people have within them the power to live better and to impose order on the chaos of their lives."
—U.S. News & World Report,
June 14, 1997

You and Only You

ONE OF THE MOST valued elements of the id for Dr. Laura is self-reliance. This is a constant theme on her talk show. The importance of depending on oneself is scattered throughout her books, her newsletters and her web page. In chapter 5 of *Ten Stupid Things Women Do to Mess Up Their Lives* ("Stupid Cohabitation"), Dr. Laura comes right out with it: "You and only you have the power, the sole power, to make you happy."[1]

Dr. Schlessinger was asked an important question by *Leadership Journal:* What was the hope that she offered to callers? Her response was very revealing: "I tell them, 'This you can do. It's going to be hard and difficult and painful and embarrassing and make you sick and nervous.' "[2]

The hope she offers is the hope that comes from self-reliance. "This you can do." Dr. Laura talks a lot about the need to raise ourselves up and make things happen through determination and human effort: "Elevate yourself to being truly human."[3]

In the Old Testament story of Cain and Abel, we see a classic illustration of sibling jealousy. Abel's offering to the Lord was more favorable than that of his brother. This made Cain very angry. So God took up the matter with Cain: "Why are you angry? Why is your face downcast? If you do what is right, will you not be accepted? But if you do not do what is right, sin is crouching at your door; it desires to have you, but you must master it" (Genesis 4:6-7). Here is Dr. Laura's commentary on this passage: "God also reassures us that we do have the capacity to rise above circumstance and attain mastery over our weaker selves, attaining the nobility that has become human beings."[4]

Finding the Courage Within

Dr. Laura was advising a caller named Suzanne who was experiencing difficulty in extricating herself from a relationship with an abusive, alcoholic man. The doctor challenged her: "You have to use your courage. There's no magic here. AA isn't going to give you the courage. And I'm not going to give you the courage. Nothing and nobody has your power to do what you need to do."[5]

Linda called to discuss her extreme dependence upon men—the wrong kind of men. The problem seemed to center around her inability to make a life for herself. Dr. Laura offered some blunt advice: "You'll have to get off your tush and have the courage to create something in this world that you can look at and be proud of."[6]

Self-reliance and Values

A young woman called the *The Dr. Laura Show* to confess that it was easier to talk about the value of virginity before marriage than it was to remain pure before the wedding. She was asking Dr. Laura for advice on "how to stay a virgin." The doctor offered this analysis:

> Values only have the power you infuse into them
> with your respect for them and yourself, and your
> will. Values without temptations are merely lofty
> ideas. Expediting them is what makes you, and
> them, special. That requires grit, will, sacrifice,
> courage, and discomfort. . . . The measure of you as
> a human being is how you honor the values.[7]

Note carefully the words and phrases used here: "the power
you infuse into them"; "that requires grit, will, sacrifice": "how
you honor the values." This brings us back to the title of this
chapter: "You and Only You." Dr. Schlessinger is radical in her
belief that human beings have everything they need to cope
with the many problems of life within themselves. According
to her, we can and must rely on ourselves for the courage, wisdom and strength to manage our daily lives.

Begging Dependence

How does this strong emphasis on self-reliance compare
with what we find in the Bible? Jesus Christ had a very different
viewpoint. In His famous Sermon on the Mount, He said:
"Blessed are the poor in spirit, for theirs is the kingdom of
heaven" (Matthew 5:3). In a book I coauthored with David
Johnson, *Joy Comes in the Mourning,* we point out the meaning
of "poor in spirit": "Defined bluntly, 'poor in spirit' means,
'with reference to the spirit, a poverty.' The Greek word is
ptochos, and its expanded nuance includes 'one who is reduced to
begging dependence; one who is broken.' "[8]

Jesus tells us that a truly meaningful and fulfilling life will be
the experience of those who do *not* rely on themselves. We must
realize that we don't have the answers. Or the wisdom. Or the
strength. Or the courage. So we humble ourselves. We choose a

mentality of begging dependence upon God. This is quite different from Dr. Laura's emphasis on looking to ourselves.

Christ denounced the fantasy of self-reliance with a single sentence: "Apart from me you can do nothing" (John 15:5). Paul framed this same reality in the positive: "I can do everything through him who gives me strength" (Philippians 4:13).

Essentially, we have here an "all or nothing" proposition—with the Lord Jesus we can do all things; without Him, we can do nothing. Though this truth is devastating to the id, it is liberating to the heart and soul. Consider how the apostle Paul's sense of powerlessness became his very source of power. God allowed a "thorn" in his life that was a continual reminder of his need to depend completely on Christ (see Second Corinthians 12:7). Paul summarized what the Lord showed him:

> But he [the Lord] said to me, "My grace is sufficient for you, for my power is made perfect in weakness." Therefore I will boast all the more gladly about my weaknesses, so that Christ's power may rest on me. That is why, for Christ's sake, I delight in weaknesses, in insults, in hardships, in persecutions, in difficulties. For when I am weak, then I am strong. (2 Corinthians 12:9-10)

Paul utterly renounced self-reliance. God allowed him to come face-to-face with something that was impossible for him to handle. It was only in his complete reliance on the Lord that he was able to find victory and peace. Like Jacob's hip displacement (see Genesis 32:22-32), the apostle experienced a "friendly wound." Christ wanted Paul to be and to remain dependent on Him.

In many ways, Paul expressed the joy and liberty of relying solely on the Savior:

[T]hrough Christ Jesus the law of the Spirit of life set me free from the law of sin and death. (Romans 8:2)

[T]his happened that we might not rely on ourselves but on God, who raises the dead. (2 Corinthians 1:9)

I have been crucified with Christ and I no longer live, but Christ lives in me. The life I live in the body, I live by faith in the Son of God, who loved me and gave himself for me. (Galatians 2:20)

For it is we who . . . worship by the Spirit of God, who glory in Christ Jesus, and who put no confidence in the flesh. (Philippians 3:3)

. . . Christ in you, the hope of glory. (Colossians 1:27)

In a persuasive criticism of Dr. Laura's "do-it-yourself" advice, Joel Belz notes that God's grace is the crucial missing element:

It's one thing to be firm, direct, and blunt with a counselee. But to be firm, direct, and blunt without offering genuine hope is to go beyond rude and become cruel. Without a message of biblical grace, you might say it is heartless to call people to righteous behavior . . . hers is not finally a workable substitute, for it calls people to do that which they cannot possibly perform. . . . Only God's grace so equips us. Only God's grace allows us to humbly look at ourselves and say bluntly: "I'm not going to make it on my own. I need help. Specifically, I need God's help to keep God's standards."[9]

Such dependence does not absolve us of our personal responsibility to take care of the human side. We are exhorted to "keep in step with the [Holy] Spirit" in Galatians 5:25. We are to "work out" our own salvation while at the same time recognizing that "it is God who works" in us "to will and to act according to his good purpose" (Philippians 2:12-13). Relying totally on Christ for everything we need does not remove our volition.

Dr. Laura would define willpower as "my will coupled with my power." But the Bible declares that true willpower is defined as "my will coupled with God's power." This is an important distinction in the two definitions. It is also a crucial balance to understand and strive for in our lives. Though we do not rely on our own strength, wisdom and courage, we are responsible to do the right thing as we are empowered by Christ. The apostle Peter reminds us that "His divine power has given us everything we need for life and godliness through our knowledge of him who called us by his own glory and goodness" (2 Peter 1:3).

Theistic Humanism

Dr. Laura Schlessinger espouses what I would call a modified or theistic humanism. Though she is firm in her belief in God as a "higher power," her written and verbal advice make one thing perfectly clear: God has pretty much left us alone to work things out. Though she would concede that our strength, wisdom and courage are God-given in a general sense, human beings are the ones that must make it happen.

Throughout Scripture, we see time and again how men, women and young people tried desperately to rely on themselves. The results were disastrous. Times have not really changed. Today, in our arrogance and defiance of the Lord's absolute right to be our Master, we insist that we too have within ourselves what it takes to lead a happy, meaningful life. But it didn't work thousands of years ago, and it won't work now.

We were created to live in "begging dependence" upon our Creator. There is no shame in that. It is the glorious privilege of each and every human being.

Marriage and Family Matters

Being a woman of the "baby boom" generation, Dr. Laura has taken some surprising and controversial positions with regard to certain marriage and family issues. With humor and courage, she challenges at least one parent to "stay at home," she denounces abortion while celebrating adoption and she highlights the sometimes stark differences between men and women. Fasten your seat belt. The ride ahead is a wild one!

"When I was very young and we had no money at all, my mom would not, no matter what, stop being at home with me."
—Deryk Schlessinger

Stay at Home, Mom (or Dad)

DR. LAURA PROBABLY TAKES more heat among women's groups for her position on stay-at-home moms and dads than any other issue. In fact, she openly states that she is going to try to convince all nannies to get another profession to force parents to parent their own children. She knows from personal experience that it is not always an easy decision to stay home. Her son Deryk tells the story with the candid jocularity of a child:

> When I was very young and we had no money at all, my mom would not, no matter what, stop being at home with me. She wouldn't go to work and leave me. So when I was a little bit bigger, she got a job at a tiny station, and I was right below at a little school. I'd get a hot dog and go up to my mom's room and say "hi." So she never left me.[1]

Excuses, Excuses

Dr. Laura has heard all the excuses used by couples who insist that both must work. She has discovered some interesting things about the backgrounds of those who often protest the loudest. In her book *Ten Stupid Things Women Do to Mess Up Their Lives*, she refers to a rather raucous response to a speech she gave to working moms. They only gave her a fifty percent approval rating! "The room seethed with hostility as I endorsed the absolute necessity of babies being with mothers and/or fathers who attend to them and provide the love and positive feedback they need to grow and mature. . . ."[2]

The makeup of her audience turned out to be quite interesting. Many of the women who attacked her were those who had "made babies with bums" who proceeded to desert them. Some gave birth as the result of a one-night stand. Others chose husbands with serious mental and emotional hang-ups. Women like this were complaining that Dr. Schlessinger just didn't understand the fact that society and social services had failed to provide for their troubled lives.

As could be expected, Dr. Laura jumped all over that. She made it perfectly clear that she was not about to take responsibility for their poor choices in a mate. But she also stood ready to discuss the need for creativity and determination in finding a way out of their various nightmares.

Shortly after this difficult speech, at another public appearance, a young woman approached Dr. Laura. She had attended the lecture described above. This mother openly admitted that she had been among the angry ones. Then it dawned on her: The resentment was an effort to affix blame on someone else. She decided on a new course. The woman created a gourmet lunch delivery service. Operating out of her home, she was able to be with her child. It was quite a change in attitude: "She had started out resenting me bitterly. Now she was thanking me sincerely."[3]

The Politically Incorrect Dr. Laura

Dr. Schlessinger is very impatient with those who would imply that there is essentially no difference between institutionalized child care and children being raised by mom or dad:

> I can't believe how many women, for example, actually want to buy the politically correct (and dangerous to our children) nonsense that institutionalized day care by strangers is equal to or superior to a mother's or father's loving attention and presence.[4]

With a touch of dark humor, she exclaims: "No research indicates full-time day care is better for children than families, unless of course it's the Manson family."[5]

In *Ten Stupid Things Men Do to Mess Up Their Lives,* Dr. Laura tells the story of an editor, his working wife and their nanny. The alarm sounds off at 5:45 a.m. By 6:45 they're downstairs for breakfast. Around 7 or 7:30, the two-and-a-half-year-old toddler comes down to greet the nanny. Meanwhile, Mom and Dad rush to catch the 7:48 train to work. Nanny and toddler spend the next eleven hours of quality time together.

Somewhere between 6:30-7:00 p.m., Mom gets home to "relieve" the nanny. Dad comes in shortly thereafter. Dinner is prepared and consumed by 8:30 p.m. Then the ritual of putting the toddler to bed begins in earnest. Mom and Dad are exhausted. (By the way, Mom is eight and one-half months pregnant with child number two.) "I don't know how we're going to do this when the new baby arrives," she states. When Dr. Laura asked this couple why they choose to live like this, they offered this bizarre rationalization: "Getting ahead and wanting to give your children more opportunities than you had is a cornerstone of the American Dream."[6]

The doctor's response offers some very insightful commentary on the American "nightmare" to which these parents had actually subscribed. What time had this couple really allotted for family? The nanny had become their child's primary emotional relationship while their lives were focused almost exclusively on their colleagues. Do they not realize just how utterly selfish they had become? Then, with biting sarcasm, she asks her readers: "Do they actually believe that a two-and-a-half-year-old child is warmed and comforted today by the future financial opportunities afforded by inheritance? Who are they kidding?"[7]

Nightmare Indeed

Attacking the root of the problem for many two-income marriages, Dr. Laura censures the notion that the so-called "American Dream" has been reduced to issues of wealth, status and self-actualization. Calling for introspection, she says: "Let's be more honest here—you want, not need stuff, just want it. And, you've bought into the new American religion of ego and acquisition. . . ."[8]

A caller named Melissa said "Amen" to the above in a sharply worded comment: "So keep on speaking the truth about people who say they don't have a choice about child care. They do; they just don't want it to seem that way. It gives their greed or misplaced values the appearance of nobility."[9]

On my way to work out at a local gym during weekdays, I pass a day care facility. I have noted something very interesting in the parking lot. The cars hustling in and out to drop off the little ones are most often quite new. I've wondered: "Are both parents working full-time to put bread on the table and provide housing or to make payments on that shiny vehicle?" As the good doctor once said, "The kid isn't going to benefit from your Mercedes five years down the line."[10]

Dr. Laura is concerned for the children who are ignored while dad and mom are earning more money to buy them more things. She received a letter from a resource specialist in learning disabilities. This person worked in her local public school district part-time in order to have more time with her three daughters, ages five, seven and ten. She told Dr. Schlessinger: "If only these parents could hear what I hear their children saying on a daily basis, things like, 'My parents don't have time for me—they don't care.' "[11]

When Ideals Are Valued

Dr. Laura is quick to admit that she often refers to the "ideal situation" for a child. During *Women's Night*, a radio broadcast, the issue of child care came up. Dr. Schlessinger painted the picture of a two-parent family, no full-time or part-time day care until the child was at least three years old. She was immediately treated to angry rhetoric. The women were complaining that Dr. Laura was living in the fantasyland of ideals. But she astutely remarked that: "The real problem in that room was that the ideal was not valued. When the ideal is valued, people make the sacrifices and efforts necessary to try to reach it."[12]

That last statement is a winner. Unfortunately, many of us are not willing to make the strenuous efforts and sacrifices that are required to bring about the ideal. This should make us wonder just how much we value the ideal.

One young mother decided to reach for the ideal and wrote to Dr. Laura about her experience. As a twenty-four-year-old mother of two boys, three years and five months, she thought she could just go back to work. She tried it for six months. But she discovered something she never expected. It was torture for both mother and child! She quit. Though it was costly in many ways, she saw the ultimate benefit of her decision: "But I have the treasure of being with my boys as they grow up. IT WAS THE BEST DECISION OF MY LIFE!! I love being their mama."[13]

Busy at Home

Dr. Schlessinger is challenging what has become one of the greatly cherished rights of parents throughout North America—the right for both mom and dad to work full-time in order to maintain a certain standard of living regardless of any impact this may have on the children. Many factors have contributed to this relatively new way of thinking.

Certainly the women's rights movement has promoted this mind-set by seeking to "liberate" women from stereotypical roles which implied subservience to men. It is an attempt to erase the TV images of apron-clad mothers baking cookies on shows like *Leave It to Beaver* and *Father Knows Best.* It is a reaction to once-popular mottos like, "A woman's place is in the home."

Also, the stakes have been raised considerably as to what constitutes the American Dream. The size of one's home, the number of toys and the number of garages in which to put the toys is becoming more and more out of reach for the middle class. Two parents employed on a full-time basis would seem to be a minimum requirement if one is to "keep up with the Joneses" in these times.

Who is right in this heated debate? Can both mom and dad work forty or fifty hours a week, trusting the care of their infants to strangers and suffer no long-term negative consequences? Or should every sacrifice be made to ensure that at least one parent is home with the children? What about a parent's right to freedom? Dr. Laura quotes a PBS *Frontline* special in which a sociologist, Dr. Sarah McLanahan, clarified this issue: "Freedom and family commitment are mutually exclusive. You do surrender some of your freedom when you undertake the care of children and promise fidelity to a spouse."[14]

As I search the Scriptures, it seems to me that the Bible would come down on the side of Drs. Schlessinger and McLanahan. The choice to have children will replace our freedom to choose other things. "Having it all" is just another myth in an arrogant society that wants to live without any restraints. Consider the following mosaic of verses: Paul tells the older women to teach the younger women ". . . to love their husbands and children, to be self-controlled and pure, to be busy at home" (Titus 2:4-5).

The wife of noble character in Proverbs 31:10-31 is a graceful and elegant lady who seems to be operating a profitable business out of her home. She finds time to balance her duties to God, her husband, her children and her staff. Clearly, she was "busy at home." It is little wonder that "[h]er children arise and call her blessed; her husband also, and he praises her . . ." (Proverbs 31:28).

Consider several passages that talk about the parental responsibility to train, correct and instruct the children:

> Hear now, O Israel, the decrees and laws I am about
> to teach you. . . . Teach them to your children.
> (Deuteronomy 4:1, 9)

> Listen, my sons, to a father's instruction;
>   pay attention and gain understanding.
> I give you sound learning,
>   so do not forsake my teaching. (Proverbs 4:1-2)

> Train a child in the way he should go,
>   and when he is old, he will not turn from it.
> (Proverbs 22:6)

> The rod of correction imparts wisdom,
>   but a child left to himself disgraces his mother.
> (Proverbs 29:15)

> Fathers, do not exasperate your children; instead,
> bring them up in the training and instruction of the
> Lord. (Ephesians 6:4)

As we look over this impressive lineup of verses, one thing becomes extremely clear: At least one parent will need to be home with the children during the formative years if we are going to be able to fulfill these biblical mandates. This kind of wisdom, teaching and correction cannot be imparted by day care workers—even if it is church-sponsored. Why? Because God has declared that He uses moms and dads for this purpose.

Of course, both divorce and the death of a spouse bring about the difficult circumstance of single parenthood. This obviously presents an intense set of challenges for the mother or father who is left alone to both raise the children and earn a living. Our communities need to surround people like this with sensitivity, prayer and financial support. In one of many passages along this line, Paul urges compassion for widows balanced with practicality: "If any woman who is a believer has widows in her family, she should help them and not let the church be burdened with them, so that the church can help those widows who are really in need" (1 Timothy 5:16).

James reminds us that "pure religion" is proactive religion: "Religion that God our Father accepts as pure and faultless is this: to look after orphans and widows in their distress and to keep oneself from being polluted by the world" (James 1:27). It is easy enough for those of us on the outside to tell every single parent with small children to remarry as soon as possible. But this advice could lead to disaster if someone rushes into another marriage just to have a mother or father for his or her child. Certainly, there are other important factors to take into account. No one should feel hurried into this critical decision.

Due to cultural as well as other considerations, it would be difficult to build a biblical case for the mother always being the one who must be home with the children while the father is earning a living for the family. It is true that mom has the unique ability to breast-feed. And she seems in most cases to be more nurturing by her very God-given nature. But there may be times and seasons in a family where a stay-at-home dad is just as appropriate. In any case, we need to establish the priority of the consistent, day-by-day presence and influence of a mother or father in the life of young children.

When is it OK for the stay-at-home spouse to return to work? Dr. Laura hints that by age three a parent could work part-time. Others would say that mom and dad should wait until the child is in all-day school. No hard-and-fast rules can be established here. Even the wide differences in emotional makeup from child to child may dictate a distinct approach for each one.

Seek First His Kingdom

Jesus said: "Seek first his kingdom and his righteousness" (Matthew 6:33). Part of seeking first His kingdom will most certainly be giving our families high priority. As one of ten children raised in a minister's home, I can testify to the blessing of having a mom who was there for me when I got home from school each day. Did we have to sacrifice some things to make it? Of course we did. But I enjoyed the happiest childhood a boy could ever want. When the youngest child, Penny, was about ten years old, my mother finished her college degree and graduated at the age of fifty. She went on to teach first grade for seventeen years to help us all get through college. All ten of us have risen to call her blessed on many occasions.

Dr. Laura's advice on stay-at-home parenting is in line with God's Word. Stay at home, Mom, or Dad.

"The time of choice is intercourse. Both men and women choose to risk the possibility of conception at that moment . . . . That the woman can legally terminate that life on a whim is a great sadness for humanity."
—Dr. Laura[1]

The Unformed Body

DR. LAURA SCHLESSINGER HAS taken a firm stand against the liberal abortion laws of our land. Once again, this has not made her popular in a culture that clings to the fantasy of sex with no consequences.

In an interview with *Leadership Journal,* a magazine for clergy, she was very bold in her denunciation of killing the unborn child. Whereas some ministers may give people their blessing to abort in special "emotional" circumstances, Dr. Laura says: "I'm absolute. I sound more like Leviticus. Unless mom is going to die (in Jewish law, if the woman is going to die, then the pregnancy has to be terminated), the fetus is a life."[2]

Tissue Samples

Dr. Schlessinger rails against the notion that the unborn child is just a mass of "inconvenient tissue." At thirty-one, a caller named Gayle was struggling with whether or not she should tell her mother about an abortion she had at the age of nineteen. It had come back to haunt her because her younger sister was now facing the same decision as the result of carelessness in an uncommitted, sex-for-fun relationship. Here's Dr. Laura: "I proposed that her sister have her baby and put it up for adoption in a two-parent family. That way, the child would not have to pay the ultimate price for his mother's moment of pleasure, passion, fantasy and obvious risk."[3]

Two Wrongs to Make It Right?

Karen called *The Dr. Laura Show* to get the doctor's advice with regard to what she called a "little bit of a dilemma." That was the understatement of the year! Karen had just learned she had become pregnant as the result of a one-night stand with a coworker. Her husband, who was infertile, was out of town on a ten-day business trip when this happened. Should she get an abortion? If so, should she tell anyone? Dr. Laura's reply was: "This is an issue of eliminating a small life to protect your reputation. There is an ironic side here. This conception took place because you wanted to sedate your pain over your brother's imminent death; the conclusion is yet another death?"[4]

Dr. Laura's point is well taken. Two wrongs (illicit sex followed by abortion) can never make a right. This is why she is always pointing callers in the direction of adoption. Even though people make mistakes by choosing immoral lifestyles, they do not have to make another blunder by aborting the resulting children. Over and over again, day after day, Dr. Schlessinger urges women to consider the adoption option. She wants to give these precious children a chance at life in two-parent homes. Only God knows how many lives have been saved by her persistent encouragement in this direction.

Sue Bohlin of Probe Ministries praises Dr. Laura for this emphasis. In her article, "Why Dr. Laura Is (Usually) Right," she says:

Another of her well-known positions is that abortion is wrong because it is killing a baby. The much better alternative is adoption. She gets particularly frustrated with women who say, "Oh, I could never do that. I could never give up my baby once it was born." Her answer to that is, "You can kill it but you can't wave goodbye?"[5]

Learning from Dr. Laura

Let me offer some examples from those who have learned some valuable lessons from Dr. Schlessinger's insistence on the rights of the unborn child.

Teena demonstrated the valuable advice she had taken to heart. She responded to Dr. Laura's discussion on the issue of abortion by recalling a recent conversation she had had with her profligate thirty-two-year-old brother. Teena asked her brother how he could have sex with each girlfriend when he knew there was the risk of pregnancy. But her brother had that all figured out. He dated only "pro-choice" women. Teena was appalled by her brother's selection process—just sleeping with women who are willing to abort his child! Teena then shared how Dr. Schlessinger had impacted her life: "Thanks to your sound statements on your radio program, I won't partake in sex at all until I'm married. . . . Thanks for encouraging me to think and act morally."[6]

Jean was forty years old and happily married with two children, ages ten and seventeen. She had just discovered she was pregnant. Jean and her husband were having a lot of doubts about continuing with the pregnancy. She dialed 1-800-DRLAURA.

Jean wanted to know how she could make such a momentous decision and then live with it. Dr. Laura pointed out that only one of those options could offer hugs and lifelong touching memories.

Then Jean acknowledged the guilt factor that would accompany the choice to terminate the pregnancy. Sensing where she was going with the conversation, Dr. Schlessinger wisely inquired, "Is your question how do you terminate without feeling bad?" Jean concurred.

Dr. Laura's response was probably not what Jean expected. She told Jean that this is precisely what feeling bad was supposed to be about. Emotional repercussions demonstrate our human psyche and spirit when we violate our conscience. Then, in her inimitable style, she told Jean: "That is what makes us special and termites not. Termites don't go into confession after they eat your house, you know."[7]

Jean decided right then and there to have the baby.

Infertile couples face many difficult decisions in this biotechnological age. A caller named Pam had entered just such a moral maze. At thirty-two, she and her husband were equally frustrated with their inability to have children. They began to read about in vitro fertilization. Pam could be implanted with four to five fertilized eggs. But the doctor explained that the procedure could produce too many embryos. The solution? Selectively terminate all but one of them. Dr. Laura highlighted the incredible dilemma posed by this scenario: "What a terrible irony: here is a woman hoping to create a life, and the road to that life will be paved with deaths."[8]

Pam eventually decided to tell her doctor that selective terminations were not an option.

James wrote a heartfelt letter to Dr. Laura after learning his lessons too late to change things. He was feeling the pain of consequences for his past promiscuity. His high school sweetheart was recovering from the trauma of aborting his child. With deep sadness, he closed by saying: "Oh yes, my child would have been five last May. I'll never forget."[9]

The Secret Place

Dr. Laura Schlessinger upholds the sanctity of life at the point of conception. She understands that the formation of human beings takes place in a "secret place" where only God can understand the when and the how: "As you do not know the path of the wind, or how the body is formed in a mother's womb, so you cannot understand the work of God, the Maker of all things" (Ecclesiastes 11:5).

This incredible lifegiving process, light years beyond our comprehension, begins with a single sperm so tiny that 1 million of them would fit on the head of a pin. When united with the egg, it culminates in a tiny, precious human being nine months later. The psalmist did his best to describe this deep mystery:

> For you created my inmost being;
>> you knit me together in my mother's womb.
> I praise you because I am fearfully and
>> wonderfully made;
>> your works are wonderful,
>> I know that full well.
> My frame was not hidden from you
>> when I was made in the secret place.
> When I was woven together in the depths of the earth,
>> your eyes saw my unformed body.
> All the days ordained for me
>> were written in your book
>> before one of them came to be. (Psalm 139:13-16)

Those of us who are committed to Judeo-Christian ethics should be exceedingly grateful for Dr. Laura's faithful support of the unborn child. She has had to endure intense reproach for taking such a firm stand.

We need to summon up the courage to become a part of the solution. We should support those organizations which reach out to unwed mothers. We should be active in adoption agencies and other groups that are seeking good homes for children that might otherwise be aborted. For too long many of us have simply proclaimed our opposition to abortion. We need to be on the cutting edge with those who offer alternatives.

*"How can you let anyone
. . . hurt your babies?"*
—Dr. Laura

For the Sake of the Children

D R. LAURA RELATES THE following remarkable story from her days as a counselor in private practice. A couple came to her with a "big secret" from their past. At first, it appeared that their problem was an inability to budget properly. They were great at getting businesses started, but because they mismanaged money, things would soon go belly-up.

Dr. Schlessinger's initial reaction was that they would be better off to meet with a certified public accountant. She certainly did not qualify as a financial advisor, but the couple insisted that she was the right person to help them.

After two sessions, and lots of going around in circles, Dr. Laura sensed that she was skating on the surface of something crucial. So she decided to talk with each one separately. When the wife came in the next week, the doctor asked her: "So what's the big secret?" She was not prepared for the answer.

When they were first married, the couple decided that they wanted to go into business for themselves. She would be his assistant. Then she got pregnant.

He was angry about the extra expense a child would bring, and the time it would take out of her being able to help him in his business. They sold the child. And with that money, he started his first business.

The woman defended the sale of the child by saying that she wanted desperately to please her husband—help him—keep him. They could always have another child. But they never did. She had always blamed herself for getting pregnant and messing up her husband's dreams. Dr. Laura was then able to comprehend the real reason for their poor financial management: "The pain and the guilt, mostly unspoken, for two decades was so great in both of these people that their self-punishing cycles of business failures suddenly became understandable."[1]

Dr. Schlessinger used this extreme illustration to make an important point about the worth of a child. A woman who is willing to sell a child to please her husband and increase his business potential just doesn't get it.

Dr. Laura had a change of heart concerning her own career and success after her son was born. She announced: "All that feminist stuff fell off of me like bad dandruff and I knew there was something more important than me and my success."[2] Now, the doctor speaks of her deep affection for her own son, Deryk: "If I had to make a choice between anyone or anything and Deryk, it wouldn't even be a choice."[3]

Don't Bless the Beast—Just the Children

A related topic—child abuse—is another subject that elicits a strong reaction in the doctor. She found herself practicing what she preaches when on one occasion courage was required to confront a beast of a father. After an exhausting day, Lew, Laura and Deryk went to a restaurant for dinner. No one was too talkative, and Dr. Laura was glancing around the room, people-watching. A family came in and sat down at the table next to them. The dad was very tall, strong and handsome. Crew cut. Probably military.

There were two small children—a young boy and his older sister who was probably eight or nine years old. The girl, wanting to sit by her mother, began to whine. Dad gruffly demanded that she next to him. The mother just sat quietly while the growing confrontation swirled around her. Obviously frightened, the child started to go where she had been ordered. As she passed by her father, he slapped her sharply in the face with his large hand.

Dr. Laura could feel her blood pressure rising. She went on the attack, saying to the man: "How could you do that? How could you hurt her like that? All she wanted to do was sit with her mom. And now I know why!"

The father was not exactly thrilled with this interruption. He got up and began to curse and threaten Dr. Laura with bodily harm. After he had blown off some steam, she turned her attention to his wimpy wife: "He's just a jerk, but how can you let anyone, any man, hurt your babies? These children came from your body. How can you let him hurt them?"[4]

Dr. Schlessinger was ultimately rescued and vindicated by the restaurant manager. He had witnessed the entire event and, along with the other patrons, was disgusted with the man's behavior. The family was asked to leave. It took remarkable courage to stand up for the sake of the children.

Dr. Laura has some straightforward advice for the wife who stays with a husband even though he is abusing the children: "It is never better—for you or your children—to be beaten, terrorized, humiliated, demoralized, or violated than to be alone."[5]

Adult Happiness at a Child's Expense

Although Dr. Laura advocates getting out of a marriage that is characterized by abuse, her advice is different for those couples that are just trying to cope with the stages, challenges and realities of life. Husbands and wives who find themselves in this scenario should choose another course altogether.

Chapter 6 of Dr. Schlessinger's book, *How Could You Do That?!* is entitled, "For Brutus Is an Honorable Man. . . . Yeah, Right (Where's Your Integrity?)." Here is Dr. Laura's take on the notion that "the children are better off with divorced parents than ones who were not happy": "Bull."[6]

Actually, that's the abbreviated version. There's more to her response. She goes on to point out two critical issues. First, research simply does not support this idea, assuming that we are not including families riddled with violence or profound substance abuse. Second, Dr. Laura reminds us that a home with the tensions and problems of folks dealing with stages, challenges and realities of life is not a toxic environment for children.

She offers proof for her second contention by pointing to the years of the Great Depression in America. Though times were extremely difficult, values prevailed. People somehow grasped that even though life was tough, physical and spiritual survival were dependent on strong attachments to family. Men and women honored their obligations. Benefit was derived from the sheer act of sacrificing and caring for children when money was tight.

Dr. Schlessinger contends that many divorced couples falsely claim that they did it "for the sake of the children." In actuality, the breakup was the result of adults seeking their own happiness and fulfillment above everyone and everything else: Mom (or Dad) wants a newer or younger sex partner. Dad (or Mom) just wants to start over. Such excuses cannot be considered to be in the best interest of sons and daughters.

The Importance of an Intact Family

Children are always better off with both a mother and a father according to Dr. Laura. This is a bold statement in our culture. A well-known example is the popular TV talk show host Rosie O'Donnell who has chosen the single-parent lifestyle. But Dr. Laura lets the chips fall where they may: "The women who determine with intent that their children shall have no father . . . are wrong—that's it, they're just wrong. They are robbing children of a father and an intact family."[7]

She offers some statistics to back up her position, facts and figures published in the *Kansas City Star,* on October 2, 1996. Children from a fatherless home are:

- 5 times more likely to commit suicide
- 32 times more likely to run away from home
- 20 times more likely to have behavioral disorders
- 14 times more likely to commit rape
- 9 times more likely to drop out of school
- 10 times more likely to abuse chemical substances
- 9 times more likely to end up in a state-operated institution
- 10 times more likely to end up in prison.[8]

Other studies indicate that 1) children raised by one parent are twice as likely to drop out of school, 2) two-and-a-half times as likely to become teen mothers, and 3) that marital status has more influence over a child's success than any other factor, including race, income and educational level of the parents.

The Myth of "Quality Time"

Do our children need "quantity time" or "quality time"? This question has been energetically debated for several decades. Dr.

Laura cuts through the smooth rhetoric on this one like a well-trained surgeon. She refers to an editorial written by Charley Reese for the *Grand Rapids Press*. Penned in December, 1996, the theme was the best gift that a parent could give his or her children for Christmas.

Mr. Reese had a friend who taught American history to sixth graders at an expensive private school. During a discussion on the Great Depression, the professor was startled to hear a student say that he hoped the United States would have another depression. Many students agreed. But why? At that time, *The Waltons*—a story about a depression-era family, was on network television. The sixth graders concluded: "If we had a depression, then perhaps our parents would spend more time with us, like they do on 'The Waltons.' "[9]

Mr. Reese then compared the time each of us has been given to a bank account from God. We are credited with a finite amount of time when we are born. We rarely know the account balance, but how we spend our time will determine our life. Parents especially need to be reminded of this tremendous truth. Few of us will come to the end and regret that we didn't work long enough hours!

Dr. Schlessinger explodes the myth of "quality time" with this one-liner (reminiscent of another recently quoted assessment): "Quality time is bull."[10]

Take an Art Class

Just in case someone thinks that Dr. Laura idolizes and coddles children, it should be pointed out that she is an avid proponent of clearly established guidelines. She believes in punishment that fits the crime. The doctor insists on teaching our young people to take responsibility at an early age.

One boy wrote to Dr. Laura and complained that his parents would not allow him to put a tattoo on his ankle. Mom and Dad thought it was a stupid idea. The son thought it was "artistic and cool," and that it was his body to do with as he pleased. But the doctor sided with the parents on this one. She pointed out that, in actuality, the young man's body was on loan from God. She concluded with this bit of advice: "Take an art class."[11]

Let the Little Children Come to Me

This emphasis on the importance and protection of children in the written and verbal advice from Dr. Laura is very much in keeping with what is underscored in the Bible. Consider these verses:

> Sons are a heritage from the LORD, children a reward from him. (Psalm 127:3)

> He took a little child and had him stand among them. Taking him in his arms, he said to them, "Whoever welcomes one of these little children in my name welcomes me; and whoever welcomes me does not welcome me but the one who sent me." (Mark 9:36-37)

> Fathers, do not embitter your children, or they will become discouraged. (Colossians 3:21)

In a world filled with abused and neglected children, we can be grateful for the strong stance which Scripture takes in defense of them. All of us are accountable before God to do everything possible to come alongside those children who are neglected or mistreated in any way.

We can also be thankful for Dr. Schlessinger's advocacy on the behalf of these little ones. She has gallantly spoken out against all types of neglect and abuse. She has fearlessly talked about the devastating impact of divorce on children in a society that has been in denial of this fact for many years. Dr. Laura has championed the vital importance of two-parent families, along with her insistence on spending both quality and quantity time with our sons and daughters.

But Dr. Laura has done more than just talk about the value and priority of children in our society. She is also doing something about it. The Dr. Laura Schlessinger Foundation was founded in February, 1998. Although Dr. Laura personally has been an avid supporter of ChildHelp U.S.A., this new foundation will also embrace and support other deserving charities serving the needs of children throughout the United States and Canada. Her mission is to involve her many sponsors, supporters and listeners in responding to requests made on behalf of these charities.

Those who may be interested in more information can write to: The Dr. Laura Schlessinger Foundation, 6520 Platt Avenue, #816, West Hills, California 91307.

Dr. Laura has reminded us in so many ways that it is worth it —for the sake of the children.

"Women are more persistently introspective
. . . men are more extraspective."
—Dr. Laura

Men Are from Jupiter,
Women Are from Saturn

DR. LAURA IS UNAPOLOGETIC in pointing out the differences between women and men. She puts it this way: "The main problem with the contemporary feminist movement (in addition to their rejection of truth or fairness) is that they simply can't stand the truth: men and women are inherently different."[1]

This fact may seem readily apparent to most people reading this chapter, but we must remember the world in which we live. The push for a unisex mentality has been with us for some time now. Many seek to blur the lines of distinction between male and female. So we should not be surprised that there has been a backlash.

With biting sarcasm, in reference to a *USA Today* survey, Dr. Laura says:

> Can it really be true that after thirty years, the women's movement has not yet reached its (unrealizable) goal of creating unisexual beings

with the same feelings, thoughts, drives, ambitions, attitudes, desires, preferences, and satisfactions? Guess not.[2]

Dr. Laura refers to an illuminating encounter between Dr. Laurence Frank, a zoologist at Berkeley, and a coed who had just heard his lecture on the way hormones determine maleness and femaleness: "In her view, 'maleness' is just macho posturing 'socially constructed' by society, 'femaleness' a myth created by the 'Neanderthal patriarchy.' But to biologists, gender is as real as oxygen."[3]

Different Wiring

Dr. Schlessinger is quick to point to respected studies that indicate the contrast between the sexes. The difference is evident at a very early age. She takes us to the sandbox to demonstrate that right from birth male and female emotionality are displayed differently. This is true because "male and female brains are wired differently, with functional gender differences on various levels."[4]

Then she elaborates on some of the ramifications of these variations. In a playful paragraph heading, she asks: "How IS a man different from a bug?"[5] Here are some of the ways she says we can see the male/female contrast in daily life.

Dr. Laura states that women are more consistently introspective. Females tend to go over and over their feelings about a problem and are able to revisit the same issue with fresh enthusiasm. But men are different: "Men are more extraspective; meaning they generally don't look at problems from such a 'personal' vantage point, but instead as tasks to be solved."[6]

She does not accuse men of having no feelings at all. It's just that they don't "lead" with emotion. One caller stated that men more often "get over" their feelings whereas women may "chew forever" on them. (Since I am outnumbered three to one in my home by my wife and two daughters, I can attest to this reality. It's just a fact of life.)

Superdad to the Rescue

Dr. Laura offers another distinction between the sexes: "Women may 'talk' instead of 'doing,' but men will 'do' instead of 'talking.' . . . It is more typically male to conquer and typically female to nurture."[7]

When Arliss, Andrea or Amanda come to me with a problem, my first instinct is to "fix it!" I'm just going to move right in and get it straightened out. "No need to discuss any further because Superdad is here!" But I am beginning to understand that sometimes the ladies in my life are just trying to express their feelings. They just want to talk with no expectation of action on my part. Dr. Laura explains why I have this tendency: "Human males have always had a typically restless attitude about new adventure, exploit, challenge, battle, etc. Human females with their more highly developed emotional empathy gravitate toward relationships, understanding and feelings."[8]

Women Existing through Men

After acknowledging and illustrating the very real differences between men and women, Dr. Schlessinger attacks the dangerous way in which women sometimes allow their entire lives to emanate from their male counterpart: "Women are so driven by the desire to exist through men that they miss the positive examples male behavior can offer them as a model."[9]

She offered a quote from Whitney Houston (*The Los Angeles Times*, 11/22/92) to prove this point. Ms. Houston said:

"Women are supposed to have husbands. We are validated by that, and we validate ourselves that way."[10] Dr. Laura's response to this statement was forthright: "It's a case of women being driven to attach to men for identity, affirmation, approval, purpose, safety, and security—values that can really only come from within ourselves."[11]

It is clear that we can indeed expect too much from the opposite sex. If we hope that our sense of worth and fulfillment will come entirely from the relationship with our spouse, we will quickly become disillusioned.

A Total Woman

Dr. Schlessinger is a great advocate of women taking responsibility for their own lives. She encourages them to refuse the role of the "little woman" who is victimized by her man. Many wives of abusive husbands are blind to their actions because of an inordinate sense of need. This is ultimately very destructive. As Dr. Laura says: "Those needy feelings create an undertow that can pull with frightening power against rationality, disgust, and guilt."[12]

All too often, says Dr. Laura, women look to men (or vice versa) for their emotional healing from past damage inflicted by a parent, sibling or former spouse. But she points out the problem with this kind of thinking: "For women to expect men to be the bandage for their hurt is to surrender the opportunity to be co-equal and confident in a relationship."[13]

She proceeds to enlighten us as to the kind of "total woman" men are really looking for:

> It's true that the good guys out there do want a total woman—not one who greets them at the front door wrapped in cellophane (on a daily basis, any-

way), but a centered, self-aware human being who wants to, rather than needs to, be with him as a companion, lover, friend, co-parent.[14]

Interdependence

Dr. Laura does an effective job of exploding the myth that men or women should be looking for their sense of completeness in a member of the opposite sex. Both male and female need to come into the relationship with a clear sense of their own worth and identity. Both should desire to contribute to the unity that results from interdependence. We can come to this conclusion, she says, by learning from the strengths of the opposite sex:

> I sincerely believe that if women studied male lessons in concepts of assertion, courage, destiny, purpose, honor, dreams, endeavor, perseverance, goal orientation, etc., they would have a more fulfilling life, pick better men with whom to be intimate, and have better relationships with them.[15]

Without a doubt, the same could be said from a male point of view. Men have much to learn from a woman's perspective. For instance, we could learn much by trying to understand how women "feel" things differently. The male gender needs to get past the selfish notion that the opposite sex is primarily responsible to comprehend their intricate personalities with no attempt at reciprocity. As men and women together move toward a greater understanding of each other's strengths and weaknesses, the possibilities for deeper love and appreciation grow considerably. As Dr. Laura puts it: "Therein lies the potential for balance and harmony: men and women, two polarities, each tempered by the unique qualities of the other, a potentially wonderful balance of outer and inner directedness."[16]

She is also energized by the incredible possibilities in the male-female relationship when this interdependence is truly embraced: "This is why I believe that men and women are at their best when they are together, tempering each other's gender tendencies, and adding a dimension of insight and energy which enriches both."[17]

She offers harsh words for those men who ignore this need for interdependence and opt for a degrading, domineering mentality. Dr. Laura accuses such husbands of insecure masculinity. Weak men like this may ignore their wives and disrespect them, but what goes around comes around. Here's her warning: "Remember . . . despots are not loved, are generally undermined, and are eventually disposed of when the time seems right. Is that the destiny you wish to write for yourself?"[18]

Male and Female Created He Them

Dr. Laura is 100 percent biblical in her emphasis on the essential difference between women and men:

> So God created man in his own image, in the image of God he created him; male and female he created them. (Genesis 1:27)

Although there were obvious physical differences readily apparent to Adam and Eve, other distinctions soon became clear. Mentally, emotionally and spiritually, men and women throughout Scripture celebrated their unique perspective as well as the particular contribution each gender made. The Bible is not just the story of great men. We are introduced to very powerful, intelligent and influential women too.

Consider just a few of them:

- Deborah (Judges 4-5) led Israel in a successful campaign against King Jabin of Hazor.
- Mary (Luke 1-2) courageously accepted her role as the earthly mother of the Savior of the world, Jesus Christ.
- Phoebe (Romans 16) was a leader and deaconess in the church at Cenchreae.
- Lois and Eunice (2 Timothy 1), the godly mother and grandmother of Timothy, were highly regarded by the apostle Paul.

Dr. Schlessinger is only partially correct in her accentuation of the fact that men and women should not look to the opposite sex for life's meaning and ultimate fulfillment. She is right on in her insistence that we should not derive our life from others or look to others for our sense of self-worth. But she is wrong when she says that we can find that sense of life and meaning within ourselves. Scripture is emphatic on this point: Humans draw their life and sense of purpose and fulfillment from Christ.

Paul wanted the Colossians to understand this great truth: ". . . Christ, who is your life . . ." (Colossians 3:4). In speaking to the Areopagus in the city of Athens, the apostle made this point: "[God] himself gives all men life and breath and everything else. . . . 'For in him, we live and move and have our being' " (Acts 17:25, 28).

Every good marriage, therefore, is the result of divine mathematics: 1 male, complete in Christ + 1 female, complete in Christ = 1. This is such an important principle to understand prior to the wedding. If we are looking to be completed by anyone or anything other than Christ Jesus Himself, we will quickly become disillusioned with our marriage. Only Christ can ultimately give us our sense of meaning and fulfillment.

Even with all of the good intentions in the world, a human spouse will sometimes fail. Jesus never fails.

Dr. Schlessinger is in line with Scripture with regard to the interdependence of husbands and wives. Though the Bible stipulates different roles for men and women in the home, Paul is emphatic that in Christ, "[t]here is neither . . . male nor female" (Galatians 3:28). As persons, men and women stand in total equality before God and each other. We are to "[s]ubmit to one another out of reverence for Christ" (Ephesians 5:21).

Just when the apostle seems to burden the wife with the exhortation to "submit to" her husband (5:22), he hits the husband with an even heavier demand: "love your [wife], just as Christ loved the church" (5:25). Peter challenges husbands to "be considerate as you live with your wives, and treat them with respect as the weaker partner and as heirs with you of the gracious gift of life . . . " (1 Peter 3:7).

Notice that Peter did not say that women *are* weaker—husbands are to treat them as if they were. The Greek word for weaker is *asthenes*. It means "physically weaker in comparative degree." It is a reference to the amount of muscle tissue. But this is not the only measurement of strength. For instance, many women are stronger than men in that they have a much higher tolerance for physical pain. Women, on the whole, also live about six years longer than men do. What Peter is talking about is attitude, not actuality.

Overall, Dr. Laura compliments the biblical themes surrounding the differences between men and women and the practical implications of those distinctions in everyday relationships. It is clear that she enjoys being a woman, and she celebrates her uniqueness in God's creation.

Indeed, this radio psychologist is a breath of fresh air in a world that is desperately trying to create a unisexual society.

Sexual Mores

After listening to *The Dr. Laura Show* for a few months—five days a week, three hours a day—I did an informal analysis of the calls to her program. Approximately seventy to eighty percent of callers are asking questions, telling stories or making confessions related to sexual mores.

Adultery, pornography, premarital sex, the difference between sex and love, homosexuality, prostitution—she has some intriguing things to say about each of these matters.

Let the reader be warned: Dr. Laura presents these issues both in writing and on her radio show with amazing candor. Some quotations may be offensive, but the author felt it was necessary to include them for the sake of a fair presentation of her views.

"A solid marriage is built on respect for the character of one's partner, not 'warm fuzzies.' "
—A listener named Mark

Sex vs. Love

NINETEEN-YEAR-OLD MARIA was having sex with a guy who told her that he doesn't love her nor does he want to marry her. But she can't stop seeing him. Maria lives in a fantasy world where she assumes that her guy must love her because of their physical relationship. Dr. Schlessinger explains how this young woman began to think this way: "Maria told me she never felt love from her parents and that the only moments she thought she'd ever experienced as love were those sexual moments."[1]

This young woman was caught in a vicious circle. She didn't feel loved or lovable. Maria had sex in order to feel loved. But later she realized it was only sex—not love.

Understanding the difference between sex and love is, according to Dr. Laura, a critical factor in determining the quality of a relationship between a man and woman. The caller quoted above, Maria, was in the grip of a powerful delusion. Dr. Laura describes what can happen: "Sexual gratification, sexual attraction, sexual feelings are tremendously powerful inducements to behaviors that seem to propel us out of control of our good sense or values."[2]

This seduction leads to obsession as the main focus becomes the perceived or actual gratification. It is that kind of excitement which can overwhelm our willingness to make wise, moral choices.

Like wearing someone else's glasses, the ability to see clearly is no longer in our control.

In her own humorous way, Dr. Schlessinger describes the ultimate disillusionment of such blinding excitement in terms that every parent of toddlers can easily understand: "If you're expecting a Toys R Us™ existence forever, you're going to have a meaningless life. If you expect that love is a feeling you're supposed to get, or that horniness is meaningful in a long-term relationship, you're wrong."[3]

Immature Lust, Mature Love

Dr. Laura beautifully and accurately describes the fundamental differences between immature lust and mature love. She portrays sexual passion as a consuming "feeling." A person cannot work, think, sleep or do anything without being cognizant of this distracting tidal wave of visceral emotion. In contrast, "mature love puts sexual passion in a context and perspective that is less all-consuming. . . . Real love is a long marination of qualities. . . ."[4]

For those who enjoy marinated chicken or beef, this analogy works. When the meat is given time in the proper environment of seasonings, the end result is delectable. So it is with genuine love. Courtship, free of sexual activity but full of the right seasonings, is the opportunity to share the delectable. As our affection for our partner-to-be or our spouse is allowed to marinate in the sweet spices of respect, admiration, appreciation, etc., the result is an even deeper love. Couples thus seasoned will make good decisions based on intellectual rather than emotional criteria: "I'm asked all the time about whether decisions in relationships should be made from the head or the heart. You can guess my answer—the head, always. Because the heart is notorious for having a more blurry picture of reality."[5]

A listener named Mark, quoted at the beginning of the chapter, wrote to Dr. Laura about his marital slump and what he had learned about sex versus love. "The fuzzies will be there, but they are not a foundation, they are a reward for depending on the true foundation: the actions of love, the honor of respect."[6]

The Waxing and Waning of Love

Dr. Schlessinger openly admits that it takes a lot of work to maintain the commitment of marriage. Part of that work is getting through those times when the feelings of love are seemingly in remission. The simple fact of the matter in married life is that "neither love nor sexual attraction is enough to ensure monogamy. Feelings of love and sexuality wax and wane with your blood sugar, moon spots, job success, hairline, etc."[7]

This is why couples need to hang in there and be willing to work toward a deeper love and a healthier relationship. Love and marriage will mature as a result of weathering storms together—not in spite of going through tough times. Dr. Laura says that this is why commitment is so desperately needed.

In this regard, notes Dr. Laura, society, religion and the state have been a big disappointment. Marriages are too easy to get into and out of—she believes that six to nine months of premarital counseling should be mandatory. As a general rule, she says that couples should date a minimum of two years before getting married.

She also attacks the ridiculous notion of no-fault divorce which has led to the quick, easy and cruel abandonment of spouses and children. She rightly asserts that the stigma that used to be attached to shacking up and extramarital affairs has vanished into thin air. Some people seem to change partners as often as they change the oil in their car.

Talk-radio's queen then goes on to describe the "mature phase" of love in contrast to the "infatuation phase." During infatuation, we gaze romantically at each other. There is a strong sense of physical attraction. This is important, Dr. Laura emphasizes, because it keeps us connected long enough to develop a more meaningful relationship based on more important things like character. But sometimes even mature love can be disappointed with the decline of fantasy and the advent of reality. Dr. Schlessinger explains it this way: "It is not that romance, affection, and passion actually disappear. It is, rather, that they are now specific to real personalities and real situations and circumstances."[8]

Taking on the role of storyteller, she goes on to tell us what happens when a woman first meets a man. She checks out his shoulders. The laugh lines. The way he moves. She notes his style of speech. Perhaps even the way his clothes fit and where! This is the fantasy part. Later, however, she discovers that this same handsome hunk wears faded, torn underwear. The dream explodes. But what would happen if she discovered that he did not replace his tattered underwear so that he could save up and buy her a new watch? She's moved to an even deeper passion.

Remorse in the Reaping

Anyone who has listened to *The Dr. Laura Show* cannot help but be touched by the remorse of those who confused sex with love. Dr. Laura's books are filled with touching testimonials from people who had to reap a bitter harvest for a life sown in lustful pleasure. Dennis offered one of the more poignant confessions.

He was a young man who promised anything just to get a woman in bed. Dennis had completely lost sight of what really mattered—things like mutual respect, goals and ideals which combine well with spirituality, honesty and integrity. He summarized the high cost of his promiscuity this way: "I have paid well for the sins of the skin and immediate gratification . . . and the pain I caused others."[9]

Numerous people share heartbreaking stories about divorces, sexually transmitted diseases, affairs and other traumas brought on by the distortion of sex = love.

A Biblical Contrast

Dr. Laura runs parallel to a biblical contrast with regard to the inherent disparity between sex and love. In First Corinthians 13, known as "The Love Chapter," Paul describes in verses 4-8 what true love is, and by implication, what it is not—lust:

True love is . . .	Sex/lust/infatuation is . . .
Patient	Impatient
Not envious	Envious
Not proud	Proud
Not rude	Rude
Not self-seeking	Self-seeking
Not easily angered	Easily angered
Not delighting in evil	Delighting in evil
Rejoicing in truth	Rejoicing in deception
Protective	Destructive
Trusting	Suspicious
Hopeful	Hopeless
Long-lasting	Temporary
Never fails	Always fails

In the stark (and sometimes dark) contrast between the sinful nature and the fruit of the Spirit, the apostle talks about the old nature in terms of "sexual immorality, impurity and debauchery" (Galatians 5:19). But the person who exudes the fruit of the Holy Spirit will display "love." That love will be demonstrated through "joy, peace, patience, kindness, goodness, faithfulness, gentleness and self-control" (22-23).

All of the elements of the sex vs. love dichotomy can be seen in these descriptions—fantasy vs. reality, short-term pleasure vs. long-term commitment, selfishness vs. selflessness, etc. Stern warnings are offered in Scripture with regard to those who continually give in to the sensual side of the carnal nature. Paul describes them like this:

> They are darkened in their understanding and separated from the life of God because of the ignorance that is in them due to the hardening of their hearts. Having lost all sensitivity, they have given themselves over to sensuality so as to indulge in every kind of impurity, with a continual lust for more. (Ephesians 4:18-19)

A Radio for King Solomon

We could wish that King Solomon could have had a radio to hear *The Dr. Laura Show* over his favorite station there in Jerusalem. Perhaps more than any other biblical character, Solomon was consumed and controlled by lust:

> King Solomon, however, loved many foreign women besides Pharaoh's daughter [his wife]. . . . They were from nations about which the LORD had told the Israelites, "You must not intermarry with

them, because they will surely turn your hearts after their gods." Nevertheless, Solomon held fast to them in love. (1 Kings 11:1-2)

Statistics reveal that Solomon could have slept with a different woman every night for almost three years! (He had 700 wives and 300 concubines; see First Kings 11:3.) But the cumulative effect of his sojourn in sensuality was that "his wives turned his heart after other gods, and his heart was not fully devoted to the LORD his God" (11:4). Essentially, Solomon sold his soul for sex. In lamenting this fact in Ecclesiastes, he admitted that not even one of those 1,000 women could satisfy the deep need of his soul (Ecclesiastes 7:26-29).

I would have loved to have heard that conversation if Solomon could have just called 1-800- DRLAURA.

Dr. Laura Schlessinger enlightens all of us who want to get a clear picture of the difference between sex and love. In doing so, she reflects key biblical principles.

"One subject upon which she and many of her trenchmates in the culture war differ is homosexuality, of which she is tolerant. But her tolerance has limits."

—Arsenio Orteza[1]

Adam and Steve

IN RECENT YEARS, MANY articles have appeared in newspapers across the country regarding the battle over the issue of homosexuality in several mainline denominations. Here is an example taken from an Associated Press news release, March 14, 1998, Kearney, Nebraska.

"A Methodist pastor was found not guilty by a panel of four female and nine male ministers Friday of disobeying church rules for performing a lesbian unity ceremony." Little wonder that there is so much confusion about this matter among those who do not attend church when pastors and parishioners are unable to reach a clear biblical position. Just where does Dr. Laura Schlessinger stand on the gay lifestyle?

In *The Dr. Laura Perspective,* she, as editor-in-chief, included an article entitled "A Pound of Cure." It was written by a homosexual named Michael Van Essen. Evidently, Dr. Laura included this in her magazine because of the teaser title on the cover: "A Gay Man's View on Sexual Responsibility and AIDS." His writing begins with this: "I am a gay man. I am emotionally and sexually attracted to other men. I have been since long before I ever knew or understood anything about sex. I offer no apologies, make no excuses, nor do I, any longer, hide in any closets."[2]

No Distinction

In a rather matter-of-fact manner, Dr. Schlessinger includes the stories of gay men and women in her books. The problems that homosexuals face in their "love lives" are treated by Dr. Laura in the same manner as that of heterosexuals. No distinction is made. No sense of shock is expressed. In *Ten Stupid Things Women Do to Mess Up Their Lives,* she tells the story of Linda and her lover/girlfriend:

> Linda was involved with another woman, a twenty-four-year-old, who had informed her that she didn't love Linda and wanted to see other people. But Linda was finding herself unable to let go. I pointed out to her that the issue really was not one of letting go of her lover but of not being able to hold on to herself![3]

Gays and Parenting

Dr. Schlessinger shared an interesting letter from a lesbian who wanted to be a parent. This woman had been a faithful and supportive listener for years. But she suddenly changed her opinion and was furious with Dr. Laura for saying that lesbians should not make babies, but could adopt other children who are homeless. Exasperated, she said: "This is the first time in all the years of listening to you in which I disagree with you. . . . I don't understand how you could ask me to give up such an important part of my life and love (having a child) in the best family unit I could provide."[4]

Dr. Laura's response demonstrates the difficult position she finds herself in by being tolerant of the gay lifestyle. Rather than address the real problem, which is the total disregard for God's structure of the family, she is left to comment on the "best interest of the child" and "socialization" issues. The doctor then refers to lesbians as "decent people, who mean to be and do their best." She says that the child is "likely to be heterosexual," implying that it could be "born" otherwise. Dr. Laura is also quick to point out that she is not making an "anti-lesbian statement."[5]

An Evolving View

That was in 1996. Since then, the queen of talk radio, in a careful, loving way addressed some mistakes in her approach to homosexuality. Read on.

In an Internet article concerning "Why Dr. Laura Is (Usually) Right," Sue Bohlin of Probe Ministries includes an addendum entitled, "What about Dr. Laura's Views on Gays?" Ms. Bohlin held out the hope that Dr. Schlessinger may change her view to a more biblical stance:

> It would appear that several years ago, she believed that people are born gay, which would remove any moral aspect to one's sexual behavior. But she has now said that she thinks something goes wrong somewhere along the way, whether it's environmental or physical, causing people to experience homosexual desires. . . . I think there is a good chance her views will become more and more biblical.[6]

My first reaction was to disagree with Sue Bohlin's assessment for two reasons. First, Dr. Schlessinger had assumed an agnostic position on this issue. Departing from many of her colleagues in psychological circles, she believes that it is impossible to understand the mysteries of gay thinking and behavior. During a moment of on-air frustration one day, she said: "This is a reality—there is no explanation for homosexuality."[7]

And in reference to her consternation with regard to the gay issue, she jokingly said: "It's something God and I will work out later."[8]

Second, for Dr. Laura to shift to a more and more biblical stance, she would be required to admit that she has been wrong all along and face the considerable wrath of the gay community. This is not to imply that Dr. Schlessinger would be unwilling to admit a mistake. She has proven time and again that she can take the heat of criticism from many fronts. I did feel, however, that this was such an area of confusion for her that she would not want to cause an uproar over an issue that she did not fully understand.

Well, I was wrong, and Sue Bohlin was right! As I listened to the show, it became clear that Dr. Laura was indeed experiencing a change of heart. On August 6, she read excerpts from a newspaper article which chronicled the statement on homosexuality adopted Wednesday, August 5, by the Anglican bishops at the Lambeth Conference in Canterbury, England. Here are some quotes from the Associated Press:

> The teaching of Scripture upholds faithfulness in marriage between a man and a woman in lifelong union, and believes that abstinence is right for those who are not called to marriage; recognizes that there are among us persons who experience themselves as having a homosexual orientation. Many of these are members of the church and are seeking the pastoral care, moral direction of the church, and God's transforming power for the living of their lives and the or-

dering of relationships, and we commit ourselves to
listen to the experience of homosexual people. We
wish to assure them that they are loved by God and
that all baptized, believing and faithful persons, regardless of sexual orientation, are full members of the
body of Christ. . . . While rejecting homosexual practices as incompatible with Scripture, calls on all our
people to minister pastorally and sensitively to all irre-
spective of sexual orientation and to condemn irratio-
nal fear of homosexuals, violence within marriage and
any trivialization and commercialization of sex; cannot advise the legitimizing or blessing of same-sex unions, or ordination of those involved in same-gender
unions.[9]

This statement was heartily embraced and endorsed by Dr.
Schlessinger. She spoke with a real heart of love that day on the
radio as she announced to millions the modification of her view:

Years ago, I was probably the only talk show host
on air who would take calls from homosexuals—lesbians and gays who just wanted to discuss a
given issue. Boy, did I get grief for that! Because I
was very much opposed to the hostility towards homosexuals, I pooh-poohed the warnings. I regret
today that I didn't pay more attention to the warnings. We now have laws allowing homosexual couples to adopt kids from birth as though having a
mom and a dad were not relevant. We also have
the enforcement of regulations that companies provide same-sex benefits equal to those of married
couples. This opens the door to the mindset that if
a marital covenant is not needed for gays and lesbi-

ans, it sure isn't needed for heterosexuals. Consequently we see the destruction of the core of society.

I personally have been agonizing over this. I've always told people who opposed homosexuality that they were homophobic, bad, bigoted and idiotic. I was wrong. It is destructive. This domestic partnership thing, where shacking up and lack of commitment now had benefits, has me up a wall.

I can't believe it! In the past I was too naive and too idealistic to see how this would crumble. I feel bad but I'm 51—I grew, I learned, and that's my position. I think the Anglican position is completely supportive of homosexuals. You cannot call these people homophobic. . . . It is quite compassionate and sympathetic but requires celibacy.

She concluded her comments with this powerful statement: "Sex within the context of a covenant between a man and a woman is the only scriptural, acceptable sexuality. I have to agree. . . . We all have challenges—it's how we rise to them that makes our character."[10]

"That Is Detestable"

Dr. Laura comes across with a genuine sense of compassion for the struggle of gay people. This is commendable. She has genuinely sought to reach out to homosexuals and she stands, as we all should, firmly against gay bashing of any kind.

The biblical stance on this issue is crystal clear: God did not create Adam and Steve—it was Adam and Eve. Scripture teaches that "[t]he man and his wife were both naked, and they felt no shame" (Genesis 2:25). Any other arrangement where people get naked with each other will bring shame for one simple reason—it is sin. (This would obviously include a husband or wife with someone else's spouse, a man with another man, a woman with another woman, or an unmarried couple who engage in sexual activity.)

Here's what the law of Moses says about this: "Do not lie with a man as one lies with a woman; that is detestable" (Leviticus 18:22). Could this possibly be stated with more clarity and force? I think not. If homosexuality was genetically predisposed, how could God say that He "detests" this practice? Can the Creator criticize what He Himself forced upon certain people? The fact of the matter is that there is no genetic predisposition to gay thinking and behavior. To use one of Dr. Laura's favorite words, homosexuality is a *choice*. Any other viewpoint leaves God in the precarious position of having imposed a lifestyle that He also condemns.

God's character could be another step toward a more biblical position on this issue for Dr. Laura. She believes in a loving and just Creator. It is only a short distance from this conviction to assert that He would not impose such an impossible moral dilemma on His creation. To give certain men and women desires for their own gender and then chastise them for pursuing those passions would be the antithesis of love. Deep in every human heart there is a recognition that homosexuality is a choice.

The New Testament is no less plain on the matter:

> Do you not know that the wicked will not inherit the kingdom of God? Do not be deceived: Neither the sexually immoral nor idolaters nor adulterers nor male prostitutes nor homosexual offenders nor thieves nor the greedy nor drunkards nor slanderers nor swindlers will inherit the kingdom of God. (1 Corinthians 6:9-10)

This is quite a list! Along with condemning some of what we would call the more obvious sins (idolatry, adultery, prostitution, homosexuality), Paul includes things like stealing, greed, drunkenness, slandering and swindling. Because of the verb tenses used, we know that the apostle is referring to those who have given themselves over to a lifestyle of sin in one or more of these areas. We are assured over and over again in Scripture that there is forgiveness for every trespass on this list. The ultimate question is, "Will we choose to forsake these sins, or will we allow them to become our way of living?"

As with all of the matters mentioned in First Corinthians 6:9-10, the homosexual can choose to repent of this iniquity. Such a person is not without the will to make that choice. Even when environmental factors have pushed in this direction, a decision can be made to go the other way—God's way. Once the sin has been recognized and confessed, Jesus Christ offers full pardon. Along with this, He will give the power to change the thought and behavior patterns that drive the gay lifestyle.

And please note this: Homosexuality is not to be considered a greater offense to God than other forms of iniquity. This is no doubt why Paul placed so many different kinds of evil in the same verses. All sin is reprehensible to God's holiness. All of our sins were responsible for the cruel death of Christ.

But having said that, we must be clear about the fact that the Bible declares we can understand the nature of homosexuality. We can comprehend its origins. We do know how a gay person can be liberated from this sinful lifestyle. In its essence, a man's attraction for another man and a woman's attraction for another woman is the flip side of the coin of lust.

This is where the Anglican statement quoted earlier in this chapter falls short. They talk about "persons who experience themselves as having a homosexual orientation." The implication is that no one really knows how same-sex passions get started in a man or woman. It just sort of "happens" to some people. But the Bible makes this much easier to understand.

A man (married or single) may have desires for a woman who is not his wife and want to become intimate with her. This is lust because the sexual relationship is reserved for marriage. A man may have desires for another man or a woman may want another woman. This is also a form of lust. God has plainly forbidden this relationship too. Lust is wanting that which cannot be had. In both cases, whether heterosexual or homosexual, we want what we cannot have. In that sense, the very first sin of the human race—eating forbidden fruit—is still very much alive but not so well.

It is amazing how far some of the mainline churches have gotten away from the reality of original sin. When this principle is denied, the doors are flung wide open for every kind of evil. Who could have imagined we would see not only clergy sanctioning homosexual marriages, but openly gay men and women seeking to be ordained into the ministry!

God said that we were not to eat of the fruit of the tree in the middle of the garden. Same-sex intimacy is just another aspect of that fruit. But human beings still want what they cannot have.

"Pornography and prostitution are easy ways to feel like a 'man'—in your own mind and in the fake behaviors of a hired sex partner."
—Dr. Laura

Food for the Eyes—
Starvation for the Soul

On ANY GIVEN DAY, *The Dr. Laura Show* receives at least one call regarding the damage caused to a marriage by pornography. Dr. Laura frankly admits: "Numerous female callers have complained about their men being swept away by pornography."[1]

Surveys of both the churched and unchurched population indicate that this sordid battle for the mind and soul is intensifying. The unimaginable proliferation of pornography is the direct result of a relaxed attitude in our legal system. Under the guise of the freedom of speech, every conceivable sexual aberration is now available in magazines, videos and CD-ROMS. The Internet is inundated with this insidious form of mental pollution. Child pornography is about the only taboo left.

Dr. Laura has found the correct label for this cerebral immorality: "Food for the Eyes—Starvation for the Soul."[2]

One male listener challenged her with the following rationalization:

The opposite sex is appealing to the five senses, including sight. So how can you condemn one who actively pursues stimulation of the optic nerve? Based upon the prolific dispersion of pornographic magazines, sexually stimulating advertisements and movies, it is clear that a large majority of people in this country are also voyeuristic. Do you really think this behavior is wrong?[3]

Dr. Schlessinger answers this question with some interesting research: "According to evolutionary psychologist Douglas Kenrick's research (*TIME magazine*, 8/15/94), men who are shown pictures of *Playboy* models later describe themselves as less in love with their wives than do men shown other images."[4]

A sobering letter from a listener confirmed this. A man who had become deeply involved in pornography lamented the fact that the reality never quite measured up to the fantasy. He regretted the way in which he had lost the ability to have a fulfilling sexual relationship because of the greatly exaggerated expectations which porn promises but cannot deliver. In mournful tones, he wrote: "NO one lives up to the fantasies—of course, no one could. I have had to accept the sad fact that, for me, sex has become fun only to watch, exciting to think about, but completely unfulfilling to engage in."[5]

This is a frustrating truth. Fantasy is always more graphic and sensational than reality. This is true about sex, but it is also true about many other things. For instance, many illusions await professional athletes in the wild world of sports. The fantasy is that a national championship, a gold medal or a Super Bowl ring will bring ultimate satisfaction. But that's not the reality.

In the '70s, the Oakland Raiders won the Super Bowl under coach John Madden. After the game and the interviews were over, owner Al Davis walked through the darkened locker room. Sitting in the corner all alone was one of his players, Gene Upshaw. When asked why he was still there, Upshaw said that he wanted to savor the moment. He knew that as soon as he walked out the door, it would be gone. Sports commentators would already be speculating about which team would win next year.

Adding to the disillusionment that comes when sexual fantasy doesn't live up to reality, Dr. Laura rubs more salt into the wound:

> More nameless, faceless, disconnected sexual gratification does not lead to a greater desire or ability to be close, loving, bonded, and intimate. The more you exercise one muscle, the more the opposing muscle weakens and the more out of balance you become.[6]

This is a dose of reality for those who argue that pornography actually helps deepen their relationship with their spouse. It simply cannot happen this way. Those who become enamored by such falsified photos ultimately realize that they are becoming more and more detached from reality in all of their relationships.

A Dangerous Compromise

Dr. Schlessinger offers what I consider to be a dangerous compromise for married couples who need to "jump-start" their physical relationship:

> Occasional viewing or reading of "sexy" material often helps stimulate "sexy behavior" when stress,

family, and work distractions might be stalling you in "neutral." So, as an aphrodisiac to help jump-start you and your wife—fine. As an alternative to relating on a real, meaningful, and reciprocal way—not fine. Pornography is about "getting," lovemaking is about "giving and getting."[7]

I radically disagree with Dr. Laura at this point. She does not take into consideration the male perspective. Sexual temptation and unfaithfulness in men begins with the eye gate. Most males could not view or read sexy materials while focusing on their spouse. And they would develop a desire for more to view and read. This is just our nature as men. I do not know of a single male who ever professed to be disciplined when it came to looking at pornographic materials.

There is also the issue of lusting in the heart for those models who appear in the sexy material. This is not a healthy way to "jump-start" a man who is about to make love to his wife. Images of perfect bodies, often disguised by clever photographic techniques, could lead to unrealistic expectations of our spouse. In my opinion, Dr. Laura strikes out with this piece of advice.

An Emotional Sinkhole

Humor can diffuse almost any tense discussion. When discussing a husband who had been unfaithful on many occasions, Dr. Laura told the troubled wife that she should not be so surprised that a gorilla was eating another banana! In this "animal" state of mind, he is incapable or avoiding of intimacy or trust. This is the emotional sinkhole which prostitution and pornography create. It is an attempt to

have a "relationship" in which men can feel automatically and completely wonderful, acceptable,
competent, masculine—without earning or deserving it! Pornography and prostitution are easy
ways to feel like a "man"—in your own mind and
in the fake behaviors of a hired sex partner.[8]

Thus, engaging the services of a prostitute is a quick fix in a
society that thrives on fast food, microwave ovens and
three-hour flights to Europe. It becomes the easy way out for
men who want to bypass the character and responsibility issues
inherent in a committed relationship. This is most certainly gorilla behavior.

Dr. Laura summarizes her thoughts on the pseudo-sex industry like this: "In the end, inappropriate sexual expressions
(promiscuity, affairs, porn, prostitutes) are paths to avoid becoming a fully functional, adult human man."[9]

Adultery of the Heart

From a mental, emotional and psychological standpoint, Dr.
Schlessinger has correctly analyzed the fantasy world of pornography and prostitution. She also condemns these vices on
moral grounds in her books and boldly censures them as callers
discuss the many ramifications surrounding these matters. As
usual, her case is quite compelling. And it is also very biblical.

The Scriptures clearly denounce any sexual relationship outside
of the marriage between a man and a woman: "Marriage should be
honored by all, and the marriage bed kept pure, for God will judge
the adulterer and all the sexually immoral" (Hebrews 13:4).

There is also an allusion to pornography in the Old Testament.
One of the ten commandments deals with the sin of covet-

ing—passionately wanting that which does not belong to you. As it relates to this chapter, God says: "You shall not covet your neighbor's wife . . ." (Exodus 20:17). This is obviously stated in a physical context. A paraphrase might read like this: "You should not look over the fence at your neighbor's wife and wonder what it would be like to have sex with her." Coveting, in this sense, is forming a mental image of the sinful pleasures you could enjoy with someone other than your wife.

Jesus also said some remarkable things with regard to pornography long before it plagued our world. He referred to it as "adultery of the heart": "You have heard that it was said, 'Do not commit adultery.' But I tell you that anyone who looks at a woman lustfully has already committed adultery with her in his heart" (Matthew 5:27-28).

We should note two things about this text. First, Christ teaches what Dr. Laura has also pointed out—the lust of the eyes is primarily a male weakness. Jesus did not say, "Anyone who looks at a man lustfully. . . ." No, this is a temptation with which men particularly must cope. Sexual temptation for males begins at the eye gate. We should not assume that women cannot relate at all to this kind of enticement. It is simply more common and more intense for men.

Second, adultery can be committed in the mind and heart of man without even touching a woman. This statement must have come as quite a shock to the scribes and Pharisees who had prided themselves in being able to outwardly keep the moral law of God through their own strength and determination. Jesus wanted them to know that mental unfaithfulness is equally abhorrent in the eyes of God.

The real point was this: Faithfulness to one's spouse—which includes a pure mind—can only be achieved by the radical change of heart that Christ alone can deliver. No one can pull that off apart from a spiritual transformation.

Obvious implications abound here for those who feel that they are practicing some kind of "innocent" or "safe" sex by viewing pornographic materials. It is not innocent or safe. There is no innocence because Jesus does not distinguish between mental and physical adultery. It cannot be considered safe because it usually leads to other forms of sexual sin.

This is why Dr. Laura is wrong in advising a couple to jump-start their marriage by occasional viewing or reading of sexy material. It will lead to cerebral unfaithfulness—especially for the husband.

It is little wonder that Paul tells young Timothy to "[f]lee the evil desires of youth, and pursue righteousness, faith, love and peace, along with those who call on the Lord out of a pure heart" (2 Timothy 2:22).

Generally speaking, Dr. Laura Schlessinger has blended her voice with that of our Lord and the New Testament writers. Pornography is indeed "food for the eyes—starvation for the soul."

"If you think Dr. Laura Schlessinger is judgmental,
moralistic and helpful—
you should listen to Jesus Christ!"
—Rev. Gregory Adkins
(*U.S. News & World Report,*
June 14, 1997)

Shacking Up

SEXUAL INTIMACY OUTSIDE THE bonds of marriage, with all of its agonizing fallout, is without a doubt the number one topic of discussion on Dr. Laura's national radio talk show. Her books are filled with tragic stories, thoughtful advice and emotional testimonies surrounding the issue of premarital sex. Her on-line column (www. drlaura.com), her nationally syndicated newspaper column (*Dr. Laura*) and her newsletter (*The Dr. Laura Perspective*) constantly deal with this overwhelming problem.

Leadership Journal asked her why such a large percentage of calls to her show related to sexual issues. She responded by saying that those calls were mostly about inappropriate sex. And the reason for the enormous volume is easy to figure out: Sex is an intense animal drive! People tend to think that if they are feeling "horny" they must act on that emotion ASAP. The doctor's blunt, humorous response to that is: "I try to explain that it means absolutely nothing other than the animal part of us wants to reproduce or have a jolly. That's it. But any animal can do that. Frogs do it."[1]

Dr. Schlessinger has been extremely outspoken on what she judiciously refers to as "shacking up." She has also reintroduced the word "immoral" in a culture that has been lulled into the stupor of calling things "amoral." Observe her indictment of a new "Guest Policy" at Grand Valley State University in Michigan. The students there decided that the males and females should be able to spend the night in each other's rooms. Dr. Laura lashed out with this laser-hot one-liner: "I don't understand a place of higher education promoting fornication."[2] (She definitely has a penchant for calling things by their actual name!)

Along with shacking up, she refers to premarital sex as "recreational sex." Consider the young woman who sent in this question to the Dr. Laura newspaper column. She had been dating a guy for one year. Prior to that, they had been friends for two years. She assumed a certain level of commitment, even though there was no ring and no date. Of course, they were sleeping together. The question: "Would it be fair for me to ask him where this relationship is going?"

Dr. Laura wrote this stinging reply:

> I am always surprised when two people can get naked and assume sexual positions—and later feel shy about talking. . . . If you can't talk about "love" and "commitment" (marriage), then you're not being "intimate" or "making love," you're having recreational sex.[3]

A caller named Cliff was chastised for his loose views on sexual relationships and commitment. His live-in girlfriend was diagnosed with lupus, and Cliff decided he couldn't marry her because of that. Dr. Laura gave him both barrels: "You are at the point of [being] committed to good sex, good times, good fun, good feelings. Cliff, just say good-bye. Let her get on with what she has to deal with, with the people who will stand by her."[4]

Origins of Amorality

So how did we get into this mess? How did premarital sex become an accepted behavior by so many? Dr. Laura traces the roots of this catastrophe to the so-called "sexual revolution" of the '60s. This revolution, which turned out to be more of a devolution, insisted that sexual mores were repressive. We needed to recapture a sense of healthy sexuality and sensuality. Sexual behavior became dissociated from the principles of love and commitment. The mantra, in simple, lewd terminology was, "If it feels good, do it!"

Dr. Laura reflects on this tragic trend especially as it has affected the female population:

> I believe that the women who succumbed to the Pinocchio promises of the sexual revolution didn't free up their sexuality as much as they lost the sense of specialness of that act and their special contribution to the life process and social cohesion.[5]

The sexual revolution has had an incredible impact. A minister friend of mine would summarize the overwhelming damage with this phrase—"the normalization of evil." Dr. Schlessinger has noted the alarming changes in society's view of living together before marriage since she began her radio work: "When I began working on radio some fifteen years ago, it was rare for a caller to admit she was shacking up with a guy. There seems to have been a relaxation of values and norms. Today, living-in no longer has a stigma attached to it."[6]

Six Consequences of Sex before Marriage

Through studying Dr. Laura's writings and listening to her radio program, I noted that she delineates at least six consequences of shacking up. Let's consider each one briefly.

1. Parental Disapproval. In "Dr. Laura's On-Line Column," a young woman wrote to express her dismay over her parents' attitude about a decision she made with her boyfriend to move in together before their wedding which was planned for the next year.

The parents were heartbroken. They distanced themselves. The young woman angrily argued that because she was in her late twenties, the parents should just accept her decision to shack up. Dr. Schlessinger energetically disagreed:

> You made a choice to reject the values of postponed gratification and the sanctity of sex and co-habitation within commitment—and in doing so, you have disappointed and shamed your parents. *You* made that choice. An adult accepts the consequences of their [sic] choices.[7]

Most parents are going to react in a similar fashion. Shacking up is frowned upon even by those who may have tried it themselves when they were young! This often becomes an extremely divisive issue between parents and children.

2. Poor Decision Making. Dr. Laura makes the point that couples who become physically involved before marriage will find it difficult to make rational, long-term decisions. In the heat of passion, people may "feel" things that have nothing to do with "fact." In her unique style of "humor with a sledgehammer," she says:

Sex outside of a committed relationship gives marriage the momentum to send you crashing into a wall of reality down the road because, my friend, when you're sexually involved, you're no longer steering. Decisions made under the influence [of a sexual relationship] . . . are not typically the best ones.[8]

This is a serious consequence of defying God's moral law. Decisions that will impact the rest of a person's life may be made in a context that is not even remotely connected to reality. Choosing a life's mate is no time for impaired judgment. One must have a good grip on the steering wheel!

3. Low Self-esteem. Another unavoidable cause and effect of premarital sex is low self-esteem. Dr. Laura equates a woman shacking up with a man to the ignoble concept of auditioning for his love and commitment: "Moving in with a man when you don't know how he feels is to try to make him feel something toward you. That's demeaning and stupid. It's about you auditioning."[9]

That word "auditioning" should make every single person stop and think carefully about his or her sense of self-worth. "If I am only a 'great person' because of what I can offer sexually, I must not think much of myself!" And notice that sex before marriage is not only caused by low self-esteem—it will also be the result of having premarital sex. This leads to the fourth consequence of shacking up.

4. Higher Divorce Rate. One of the ironies of living together before marriage is that it actually provides less and not more of an indicator of the quality and duration of the union. Dr. Laura cites statistical proof for this proposition. Psychologist David G. Myers, Ph.D., author of *The Pursuit of Happiness*, points to seven recent studies indicating that couples who cohabit before marriage will have a higher divorce rate than those who don't. Three national surveys indicate the same results:

- A U.S. survey of 13,000 adults found that couples who lived together before marriage were one-third more likely to separate or divorce within a decade.
- A Canadian national survey of 5,300 women found that those who cohabited were 54 percent more likely to divorce within fifteen years.
- A Swedish study of 4,300 women found cohabitation linked with an 80 percent greater risk of divorce.[10]

One obvious reason for this very high rate of divorce among those who shacked up goes back to the second consequence we saw earlier: Judgment is impaired by the sexual relationship. A man and a woman may feel that they belong together just because the physical aspect of their time together was exciting. But after marriage, when times are not always so arousing, other areas of incompatibility torpedo the ship, and the relationship sinks.

5. Babies and Other Physical Dilemmas. We are all familiar with the potential STDs (sexually transmitted diseases) that can be passed from one person to the next. In actuality, to sleep with a man or woman is to sleep with everyone that he or she has had sex with previously. Also, couples who choose to live together on a trial basis before marriage are sometimes faced with a pregnancy. Even the very best birth control methods are not 100 percent effective. News like "I'm pregnant" can change the tone of a relationship within seconds. Does the couple want to arrange for a quick marriage? Abortion? Should the child be given up for adoption while the mother and father continue to debate their compatibility for marriage?

Here's a fax that no doubt made Dr. Laura's day, month and year. This man had been a pro-choice/pro-abortion/sexually active guy for years. A recent event at his girlfriend's apartment was rather remarkable. Things were getting hot and heavy. She offered to get a form of contraceptive. But then something dramatic happened. The guy said that he wanted them to stop and think about what they were about to do. He had some heavy questions to ask.

> I stopped everything and said, "If you got pregnant and had the baby, I couldn't bear seeing my son or daughter put up for adoption. I would not want to live life knowing that the future of someone I created was to be determined by someone else. If you got pregnant and kept the baby, I would plan on being around for the next 20 years at least. Do you know me well enough to accept that now?"[11]

The young man continued to ask about the pain and suffering of the abortion option. Was she willing to risk a future without being able to have children? What other physical complications could arise through such a horrendous medical procedure?

His girlfriend began to weep. She confessed that she had never met a guy who cared about her so much. His fear of her reaction now seemed so silly. Rather than thinking he was crazy, she was even more crazy about him!

6. *Guilt and Unhappiness.* The sixth consequence of premarital sexual relations seems odd in our upside-down world today. But there really is a sense of guilt and unhappiness for those who do not save physical intimacies for marriage. Dr. Schlessinger tells us about a twenty-year-old named Zack. He had left his church and his moral convictions so he could drink and have sex with his girl-

friend. Though he was doing both of those things, Zack was not able to deaden the guilt.

The young man admitted that he would never marry this girl because "she wasn't a Christian" and his ultimate goal was to have a Christian wife and lead a Christian life. He was just sowing some wild oats while he was young and able to enjoy it fully. When questioned about why his church had rules about premarital sex, Zack gave the textbook answer: so children won't be born out of wedlock and to make the sexual relationship special. He knew that to line up with his religious training, he would have to give up both his girlfriend and the sex.

Listen to the closing dialogue between Dr. Laura and Zack:

> DR. LAURA: "Okay, Zack, to keep her and to enjoy sex you have to pay a price. What is that?"
> ZACK: "Well, I feel uncomfortable about it all. I miss some of the things about the church, but I'll get back to it someday."
> DR. LAURA: "Bottom line, Zack, is that the drinking and the sex are pleasurable right now. But, all in all, you're not too happy?"[12]

Zack answered only with silence. That spoke volumes.

Dr. Laura refers to an article from *The Los Angeles Times* (12/29/96) which reported a story about the small number of ultra-Orthodox Jews who were abandoning their faith for the supposed "freedom" of secularism. One young man who had discarded his religious life for unrestricted sex made this assessment: "My therapist told me that I would live a life of conflict, and he was d——- right. It is not easy to leave religion. . . . After you leave, you feel so deserted. Spiritually, there is a black hole."[13]

It's quite a list, isn't it? Look at the consequences of premarital sex one more time:

- Parental Disapproval
- Poor Decision Making
- Low Self-esteem
- Higher Divorce Rate
- Babies and other Physical Dilemmas
- Guilt and Unhappiness

Committed Relationships

After examining the dire consequences of a "love the one you're with" mentality, Dr. Laura celebrates the beauty of a man and a woman who are committed exclusively to each other: "Whereas biology provides the beauty and excitement of sensual and sexual pleasures, men ultimately realize that the real thrill comes from the love and acceptance from a woman in a committed relationship."[14]

She correlates this joy of covenant with spiritual and moral implications: "Two consenting adults is [sic] not nearly as spiritually elevating as two consensual committed adults."[15]

In counseling a young man who was interested in having "meaningful" sexual relationships, Dr. Laura stated: "There is something wonderful about considering sex in a more 'holy' or 'moral' light. It gives the act greater magnificence, depth, and ongoing satisfaction. . . ."[16]

Pastor Laura Challenges the Church

One of the realities stemming from the church's failure to be "relevant" is that people like Dr. Laura Schlessinger become a pastor or priest figure to millions. Fed up with hypocrisy and

scandal, many Americans have decided that the church or synagogue is not necessarily the only place to find the moral compass needed to navigate life at the turn of the century. Many
people openly talk about "following Dr. Laura's teachings" as if
she were a religious guru.

How has this happened? I believe that Dr. Schlessinger—her
books, tapes, newsletter, web site, radio program—has filled a
void for many who are seeking the truth. She is so refreshingly
bold and honest. She is appealing to the God-given ability in every
human being to know right from wrong. Hers is a voice crying in
the wilderness of an amoral nation: "Come back to your senses!
Stop behaving like the lower animals! We were created for better
than this!" Sadly, in many cases, the churches and synagogues are
no longer that voice of moral authority.

Dr. Schlessinger tells the sad story of a man who called her show
and identified himself immediately as a "born-again Christian."
He also happened to be separated from his wife and having sex
with a live-in lover. But the guilt was getting to him. Dr. Laura
asked him why he thought his church condemned sex outside of
marriage. He could only respond by saying that it was a "sin."

The doctor appealed to the bigger picture: "I am saddened that
too many pulpits don't challenge the folk in the pews (lest atten-
dance drop?) about their personal behaviors in the context of
moral choices, which ultimately give dignity to fundamentally animal behaviors."[17]

In the light of the anemic homilies that often pass for preaching
these days, Dr. Schlessinger's point is well-taken. The church has
lowered the volume on the subject of sin. And in those congregations where evil is condemned, the minister is often content to just
leave it at that. The prohibition goes no further than "thou shalt
not." We have removed wicked behavior from the context of
God's system of moral law.

For many baby boomers (who left the church twenty or thirty years ago), and for many baby busters and generation Xers (who never started going to church), Dr. Laura is the only moral map which can be navigated. Though her advice is not usually fun to follow, those who do discover that she is right most of the time. She has dared to speak passionately and openly about things that have been hush-hush in religious circles. That has won this radio talk show host the admiration of multiplied millions. To them, she is Pastor Laura.

With or without the Church

Dr. Peter Wagner, a leading missiologist from Fuller Theological Seminary, was visiting the campus of Nyack College in Nyack, New York several years ago. He praised the school's founding denomination, The Christian and Missionary Alliance, for its missionary heritage and zeal. But then Dr. Wagner uttered this profound warning against complacency: "God has a plan to reach the world with the saving gospel of Jesus Christ. And He will accomplish that plan—with or without this denomination."

This was not meant to be insulting. Dr. Wagner was simply pointing out the fact of the matter. Although Almighty God would be pleased with any group's cooperation, He does not need it to accomplish His mission in the world. If one denomination fails to do its part, God will find someone else to take its place.

As we consider the widespread popularity of Dr. Laura Schlessinger and her advice based on Judeo-Christian ethics, it is as if God is saying, "I have standards for moral and ethical behavior, and I will see to it that they are heard loud and clear—with or without the church." Make no mistake: The Lord would prefer to do this through His Church, but when pastors and parishioners fail to accept that challenge, He will find other voices. Dr. Laura is no doubt one of those voices.

There is a sense in which she has stolen the thunder that should be coming from those who preach the Bible. It is easy to excuse it all by saying, "Well, if Dr. Laura identified herself as a 'born-again believer,' no one would listen to her either." But consider this: She has identified herself as a dedicated Jew. She unashamedly tells of her conversion to Judaism a few years ago, largely as the result of her need to give her newborn son a moral framework in which to live.

We have much to learn from Dr. Schlessinger's approach to shacking up. She not only attacks the immorality of it—she also exposes the impracticality of that lifestyle and the numerous consequences of embracing amorality. Dr. Laura is not just in line with God's Word—she has communicated His moral pronouncements with humor, creativity and courage.

More power to you, Dr. Laura!

Spirituality

Dr. Laura Schlessinger offers her perspectives on spirituality through the window of Judaism. We need to carefully consider her statements in this regard. What does Dr. Laura believe about mankind's dilemma with sin? How does she say one develops a meaningful life and relationship with God? Is there a heaven to gain and a hell to shun? These critical issues must be placed under the scrutiny of Holy Scripture.

*"Neither men nor women
are inherently bad."*
—Dr. Laura

18

Inherently Neutral

ORIGINAL SIN. IT EVEN sounds unpopular. The origins of evil are being debated more vociferously today than ever before. One reason for this would be the proliferation of unthinkable crimes being committed throughout the world. We have a desperate need to understand why these tragedies occur. Causation is a key concern.

So where does all this evil come from? Here are some of Dr. Laura's thoughts on this important subject:

> I believe we are the sum total of all that we do, i.e., what we "do" is who we "are." This is true because as adults we make deliberate choices in our actions. Therefore, our actions describe our inner selves, what sacrifices we're willing to make, what evil we're willing to perpetuate.[1]

Dr. Laura offers teaching from Judaism on the subject of original sin:

> In Judaism it is said that each human being has two impulses, one for evil and one for good. That dual na-

ture means that you are neither inherently good nor bad; and you are, or become, what you do. . . . Neither men nor women are inherently bad.[2]

Reaching Our Potential as Humans

In her interview with Andrew Cohen of the Moksha Foundation, she responded to a question about the potential of human beings. Dr. Laura said that it was "to be decent. We're not innately decent. We're potentially decent or moral. It has to be taught."[3]

Mr. Cohen then pointed out that many of our philosophers and great thinkers in numerous academic circles seem to have become fundamentally cynical about the progress of mankind toward the goal of a more loving, caring race. Dr. Schlessinger responded by saying:

> I wonder if they're cynical about our potential or if they aren't depressed that we don't seem to be reaching it in their lifetime. . . . I don't think they're cynical about our ultimate potential. I think they're cynical about our current willingness to try to attain it.[4]

Dr. Schlessinger seems to think that we just need to try harder to be good, decent people. If more strenuous efforts in the direction of righteousness were forthcoming, society would see dramatic changes. Is she right about this?

Murder in the Hearts of Children

On March 24, 1998, as I was writing this chapter, a tragic shooting took place in Jonesboro, Arkansas. Two boys, eleven and thirteen years old, "carrying rifles and wearing camouflage, waited in some trees after pulling a fire alarm inside Westside

Middle School. The students were shot as they streamed out of the building."[5] Fifteen people were hit by the gunfire, and five were killed—four girls ages eleven to twelve, and one female teacher. This was the seventh such mass shooting in America between October 1, 1997 and May 31, 1998 involving kids.

Dr. Schlessinger was interviewed on ABC News' *This Week with Sam Donaldson and Cokie Roberts* with regard to this enormous tragedy. As the panel of questioners sought in vain to answer the difficult why and how inquiries, Dr. Laura said: "It's really clear that inside each person—especially children who haven't yet gone through the entire socialization process—that they have the capacity for great cruelty and great evil."[6]

As we put together Dr. Schlessinger's statements in this regard, a definite pattern emerges. She would say that humans are not inherently good or evil. Rather, we are inherently neutral, with the potential or capacity to go either way. She puts the emphasis on our need for maturity and socialization to overcome anything evil in our natures. We can, Dr. Laura contends, choose by sheer force of the will to do good things instead of bad things, and thereby earn our own righteousness.

Perhaps one factor which has greatly influenced Dr. Laura's philosophy regarding the origins of good and evil is her denial of a real devil. A woman called her show to complain about a relative who tried to tell her child that there was no such thing as Satan. Dr. Schlessinger replied: "I don't believe in Satan either. We don't need Satan. All I need is you doing crappy behaviors. Why do we have to invoke a Satan? People have free will, make a choice, and do bad things—on their own."[7]

Evidently, Dr. Schlessinger would place the devil in the same category as a ghost. It's a figment of human imagination. Perhaps it's even an excuse for wicked behavior, i.e., "the devil made me do it!" People talk about ghosts, but it's hard to pin one down and study it. So it is for Dr. Laura in regard to Satan.

I'm Not OK—You're Not OK

The Bible proclaims a radically different view. From Genesis to Revelation, Scripture declares the existence of a very real devil. And his intentions for the human race are no less than horrifying. In the form of a serpent, Lucifer tempted Adam and Eve to disobey their Creator (Genesis 3:1-7). He is later described as a "roaring lion" who roams about "looking for someone to devour" (1 Peter 5:8). Satan disguises himself as an "angel of light" to confuse and deceive us (2 Corinthians 11:14). He was personally responsible for the incredible calamities that plagued Job (Job 2:7).

Not only do we have the potential for evil—we are wicked at the very core: "The heart is deceitful above all things and beyond cure [KJV—"desperately wicked"]. Who can understand it?" (Jeremiah 17:9).

The Governor of Arkansas, Mike Huckabee, made an outrageous statement with regard to the cold-blooded murders of children by children in his state: "It makes me angry not so much at individual children that have done it as much as angry at a world in which such a thing can happen."[8]

The governor wants to somehow place the blame for this incredible calamity on "a world in which such a thing can happen." Though it is true that we live in a thoroughly corrupt society, the culpability for this mass murder still rests on the boys who did the shooting. This act arose from the sinful natures with which they were born. And everyone of us has enormous potential for evil because of this reality: "Surely I was sinful at birth, sinful from the time my mother conceived me" (Psalm 51:5).

In Springfield, Oregon, fifteen-year-old Kip Kinkel exploded the heads of both of his parents and then went to school to kill two students. A few weeks later, an editorial entitled "Blame Those Who Pull Trigger" appeared. In the article, political journalist Brian Doherty complains that the whole profession of being an expert demands complicated answers when children become murderers. He sarcastically notes, "Nothing so simple as individual evil can be considered" by the analysts. But it is often much less complex:

> The one ultimate cause of any sinister act, no matter how many outside forces of social pressure are brought to bear, is individual choice. . . . It wasn't "we" who allegedly murdered our parents and then marched into our high school cafeteria armed with three weapons and opened fire. It was one kid, the authorities say—and that kid has a lesson to learn.[9]

Though most of us cannot relate to the horrendous scenarios which have unfolded across the country, we can still understand that we too are regularly plagued by the propensity for wickedness. We may be more familiar with temptations related to sexual immorality, stealing, drugs, gossip, drinking, hatred, pride, envy, anger or selfishness. And we wrestle daily with these things. Why? Because we are inherently evil. This is the bad news.

The Bible teaches that our sense of both self-worth and sinfulness comes from God Himself. As our Creator, He has clearly revealed His thoughts about His creation. When Adam and Eve were brought into being, God said that this creative act was "very good" (Genesis 1:31). The first humans were perfect in every way. Then they succumbed to temptation. Everything changed in that instant. The human race was plunged into evil. By chapter 6 of Genesis we read:

> The LORD saw how great man's wickedness on the earth had become, and that every inclination of the thoughts of his heart was only evil all the time.

The LORD was grieved that he had made man on
the earth, and his heart was filled with pain. (6:5-6)

This is what is known as "original sin." The disobedience of
Adam and Eve in the Garden of Eden polluted the entire human
race. Every child since has been born with a sinful nature. Unfortunately, we are inherently bad. It is not that we are just capable of
doing evil—we *are* evil. Our nature is bent in the direction of rebellion. This will be true regardless of our noble intentions to do the
right thing. The psalmist declares that "there is no one who does
good. . . . All have turned aside, they have together become corrupt; there is no one who does good, not even one. . . . no one living is righteous before you" (Psalm 14:1, 3; 143:2).

Jesus declared that we were born into the wrong family. We
behave sinfully because we take after our spiritual father: "You
belong to your father, the devil, and you want to carry out your
father's desire" (John 8:44).

He also said: "[F]rom within, out of men's hearts, come evil
thoughts, sexual immorality, theft, murder, adultery, greed, mal-
ice, deceit, lewdness, envy, slander, arrogance and folly. All these
evils come from inside and make a man 'unclean' " (Mark
7:21-23).

Paul and John leave no room for misinterpretation or confusion.
We are sinners both by birth and choice: "[A]ll have sinned and
fall short of the glory of God" (Romans 3:23). "[T]he sinful mind is
hostile to God. It does not submit to God's law, nor can it do so"
(8:7). "If we claim to be without sin, we deceive ourselves and the
truth is not in us" (1 John 1:8).

And Now for the Good News

Thankfully, there is also some very good news: God sent His
one and only Son, Jesus Christ, to restore the relationship that

sin—your sin and my sin—had destroyed. We can be forgiven and declared righteous in the eyes of our heavenly Father. Listen to the apostle's celebration of this great truth:

> [J]ust as the result of one trespass was condemnation for all men, so also the result of one act of righteousness was justification that brings life for all men. For just as through the disobedience of the one man the many were made sinners, so also through the obedience of the one man the many will be made righteous. (Romans 5:18-19)

> [I]f anyone is in Christ, he is a new creation; the old has gone, the new has come! All this is from God who reconciled us to himself through Christ. . . . (2 Corinthians 5:17-18)

Our sense of personal righteousness needs to be derived from Christ and His redemptive work. We can be born again to a whole new family. We can switch spiritual fathers from Satan to God. And our new Father will see us in Christ as a totally new creature—pure, forgiven and cleansed. We can be considered righteous by our simple faith and commitment to Jesus:

> Therefore no one will be declared righteous in his sight by observing the law; rather, through the law we become conscious of sin.
> But now a righteousness from God, apart from law, has been made known, to which the Law and the Prophets testify. This righteousness from God comes through faith in Jesus Christ to all who believe. (Romans 3:20-22)

Why Does This Matter?

To answer that question, let's revisit some earlier quotes from Dr. Schlessinger from the beginning of this chapter:

"What we do is who we are. . . ."

"You are neither inherently good or bad . . . you are, or become, what you do. . . ."

We could summarize these statements by saying that "we can become good by doing good." It looks easy. It appears innocent. There is an element of truth in it. But it is not at all biblical.

Scripture proclaims that we are inherently evil. We are not programmed to do the right thing. It is our nature to break God's law. This fact cannot be overpowered by simply choosing to do good. Paul described the intense battle with sin that goes on in every human heart: "When I want to do good, evil is right there with me. . . . What a wretched man I am!" (Romans 7:21, 24).

According to Dr. Laura's philosophy of original sin, each of us must find a way to shift gears from morally neutral to morally good. We start out somewhere between good and evil, and by our own wise choices and through our own strength and determination, we attain our own righteousness. But the end result of such a pursuit will be exactly the same as it was for the Pharisees—a pleasant outward appearance with no transformation in an evil heart. Jesus said,

"Woe to you, teachers of the law and Pharisees, you hypocrites! You clean the outside of the cup and dish, but inside they are full of greed and self-indulgence. Blind Pharisee! First clean the inside of the cup and dish, and then the outside also will be clean." (Matthew 23:25-26)

Only Jesus Christ can clean the inside of the cup and dish—that is, the heart of a person. We cannot cleanse ourselves from the inherent sinfulness that plagues us. This is why the apostle Paul answered his own question in Romans 7:24 about "Who will rescue me from this body of death?" by saying: "Thanks be to God—through Jesus Christ our Lord!" (7:25).

Paul continues to celebrate this wonderful freedom from trying to create our own righteous standing before a Holy God:

> Therefore, there is now no condemnation for those who are in Christ Jesus, because through Christ Jesus the law of the Spirit of life set me free from the law of sin and death. For what the law was powerless to do in that it was weakened by the sinful nature, God did by sending his own Son in the likeness of sinful man to be a sin offering. And so he condemned sin in sinful man, in order that the righteous requirements of the law might be fully met in us. . . . (8:1-4)

Do you see why this matters? Wherever we begin with the notion of original sin will dictate where we will end with our concept of righteousness. If we are born inherently neutral, then it must be possible to attain a holy life through simply choosing good over evil. It's all up to me. It's all up to you.

However, if we come into this world inherently evil, then we have a problem that only God Almighty can solve.

In short, we need a Savior.

"In Jewish understanding, basically God is unknowable."
—Dr. Laura

To the Unknowable (?) God

THE MOKSHA FOUNDATION, LED by Andrew Cohen, is "dedicated to the enlightenment of the individual and the expression of enlightenment in the world."[1] Mr. Cohen tells the story of how, in 1997, Dr. Laura Schlessinger became the main focus of his twelveth article in a series entitled, "What Is Enlightenment?" Along with his associates, Cohen was enjoying their annual retreat in the Indian holy city of Rishikesh. As the editorial team was discussing plans for the next issue, a colleague produced a newspaper clipping from the weekly entertainment supplement of *The San Francisco Chronicle.* There she was—Dr. Laura, blond and coifed, on its full-color front page.

As his associate eagerly read the article, Cohen grew impatient. Finally, it occurred to him that his colleague wanted Dr. Laura to be the centerpiece of the next edition.

Cohen was able to uncover some fascinating and revealing information with regard to Dr. Laura's views on God, her conversion to Judaism and how she has immersed herself in those traditions.

> She confided that in her own spiritual life, she feels
> a lack of intimacy with and connectedness to God.

As our conversation continued, though, it became increasingly clear that Dr. Laura is not so much a woman of spiritual depth as a woman of faith, that her passion and conviction come not from direct spiritual experience, but from her unwavering belief in the ideas and ideals of her chosen religion.[2]

When Andrew Cohen asked Dr. Schlessinger what her concept of God was, she offered these thoughts:

In Judaism, God is not something conceivable. This messed me up a little bit because I grew up on Charlton Heston movies, in which, you know, God is a guy with sandals and long hair. But Jewishly, that's the point of the commandment regarding idols.[3]

Dr. Laura then illustrated the frustration of not being able to understand God with the story of Job. Although all of his friends gave it their best shot, no one could truly fathom what was going on in this poor man's life. Consider his overwhelming circumstances: 1) His livestock were stolen; 2) his sheep and servants were incinerated in a firestorm; 3) a tornado swept through and killed his sons and daughters. And that's just the first day!

Here's what happened a few days later, "So Satan went out from the presence of the LORD and afflicted Job with painful sores from the soles of his feet to the top of his head. Then Job took a piece of broken pottery and scraped himself with it as he sat among the ashes" (Job 2:7-8).

Dr. Laura recalled how unfair it seemed at the end of the book when God takes only about one inch of the page to offer a very unsatisfying answer to all of Job's suffering. Her best explanation was, "In Jewish understanding, basically God is unknowable. You cannot fathom the motivations. You can struggle to study. You can struggle to understand, but ultimately, it is way beyond us. I accept that, and find peace in that."[4]

Dr. Laura points out that this has not been an easy resignation for her as an intellectual. As a compulsive, highly organized individual, she would not seem to be a likely candidate for believing in a God who seems distant—even unpredictable. But she stands in awe of Jehovah, not in spite of His remoteness, but because of it.

"Behave as If God Is Your Friend"

In *Ladies' Home Journal* (April, 1998), Mary Mohler conducted a wide-ranging interview with Dr. Laura Schlessinger and Anne Graham Lotz, daughter of evangelist Billy Graham. Although it was entitled, "Are There Really Angels?," the focus was much more general—"to discuss what has made spirituality important to so many of us."[5] Ms. Mohler asked this question: "How would you advise someone who is just beginning the spiritual journey and doesn't feel that connection to God?" Observe Dr. Laura's response:

> This is where you use the "as if" technique. I tell a couple who's having a hard time, "Behave as if you really love your spouse." Likewise, behave as if God is your friend. The more you behave as if you have that relationship—the more you pray, study, meditate—the closer you come to it. You can't just wait for a revelation.[6]

When asked, "Do you feel a sense of godliness as you go about your day?," Dr. Laura replied: "It's a struggle. I talk about it on the air so listeners will understand it isn't a slam dunk."[7]

183

As Close As the Law Will Allow

It is clear that Dr. Schlessinger defines any kind of personal relationship with God in the realm of the theoretical. Because Jehovah is essentially unknowable, the best she can hope for is to get as close as possible through following the law. Strict adherence can at least offer a sense of getting closer to the Almighty. But she openly and humorously confesses her struggles with obeying the rules of Judaism:

> On Saturday no more shopping, no more this, no more that. That was a nightmare, probably the toughest thing. For me, you get up on Saturday, eat breakfast and go to the mall. All week you work your brains out: this is the reward. The first couple of Saturdays I literally stayed in bed.[8]

When she first began the discipline of eating kosher, she was overwhelmed with the loss of pork, shrimp and baby back ribs. Most likely with a wink and a smile, she said: "There better be a God, or I'm gonna be real ticked off at the end."[9]

Mary Mohler of *Ladies' Home Journal* asked, "What spiritual practices keep you on track? Do you meditate, read Scripture, read religious writers?" Dr. Laura replied, "Judaism makes this easy. As an observant Jew, I have two and a half million obligated behaviors or prayers, plus candles and more prayers, and synagogue, and more prayers. I am immersed; it's like being back in the womb."[10]

Throughout her books and writings, as well as her published and television interviews, it is clear that Dr. Laura is on a sincere quest to know God. Her curiosity is much more than the arrogance of one who taunts us by saying, "I know the Creator better than you do!" This search goes beyond the selfishness and immaturity of becoming acquainted with the Almighty in order to get more from Him. Dr. Laura truly wants to know, love and please God.

Identifying the Unknown God

Paul the apostle encountered a very similar scenario when he traveled to Athens. Like Dr. Schlessinger, the Athenians were very religious and sincere in their desire to know and understand the nature and presence of God: "I see that in every way you are very religious. For as I walked around and looked carefully at your objects of worship, I even found an altar with this inscription: TO AN UNKNOWN GOD" (Acts 17:22-23).

Along with various other idols, the religious leaders of Athens wanted to make sure that they covered all the bases by creating an altar to an unknown god. In this way, if they had somehow missed the real one, this shrine could become the catchall for the genuine article. This could also serve as the god for those who chose not to worship any of the established deities.

Rather than blast the Athenians for their homage to false gods, Paul decided to use the illustration of the unknown god to introduce the people to the one and only true God:

> "Now what you worship as something unknown I am going to proclaim to you.
>
> The God who made the world and everything in it is the Lord of heaven and earth and does not live in temples built by hands. And he is not served by human hands, as if he needed anything, because he himself gives all men life and breath and everything else.
> . . . God did this so that men would seek him and perhaps reach out for him and find him, though he is

not far from each one of us. 'For in him we live and move and have our being.' " (Acts 17:23-25, 27-28)

What a wonderful reality: "He is not far from each one of us." God wants us to seek Him and find Him! We can move beyond mere religion to an actual relationship with the Almighty Creator of the universe! David's promise to Solomon fits here: "If you seek him, he will be found by you . . ." (1 Chronicles 28:9).

Jesus assured us that good things will happen when we ask, seek and knock: "Ask and it will be given to you; seek and you will find; knock and the door will be opened to you. For everyone who asks receives; he who seeks finds; and to him who knocks, the door will be opened" (Matthew 7:7-8).

Paul pointed the Athenians to the first step in the process of seeking after the true God: "[H]e commands all people everywhere to repent" (Acts 17:30). If we want to know God, we must pursue the same course.

Anne Graham Lotz had a very different answer to the same question posed to Dr. Laura. When asked how she would advise someone who is just beginning the spiritual journey and doesn't feel a connection to God, Lotz said: "[T]he first step is to establish a personal relationship with God through Christ. Otherwise you will start your spiritual journey with the cart before the horse."[11]

God sent His Son in human form so that we would be able to know the heavenly Father on a personal level. In Christ, then, Almighty God becomes knowable!

"I would not make a vow as a Jew
that my temple is the only way to God."
—Dr. Laura

Many Ways to Truth and God?

"RELIGION, I BELIEVE, IS probably the most important component of a well-lived life, because it points out the meaning of life and—by teaching the values of cooperation, sacrifice, compassion and love—provides a road to God."[1]

At first glance, this would appear to be an innocent if not honorable quote from Dr. Laura. She talks a lot about the importance of religion and being religious. But what exactly does Dr. Laura mean by using these terms?

She tells us that religion provides "a" road to God. Does this imply that there is more than one way to know God someday? A more important question could not be asked or answered. Let's do some exploring.

Religious Tolerance . . . within Limits

A caller asked Dr. Laura how he could keep his marriage together in the midst of a conflict with his wife over religion. His wife had demanded that he take a vow stating that the religious views of their denomination were the correct beliefs. The radio talk show host offered her opinion: "I would not make a vow as a Jew that the temple—my temple—is the only way to God. I couldn't do that. Fortunately, in Judaism, you're not asked to."[2]

Roger Jones wrote an article for *The Dr. Laura Perspective* entitled "The Six Stages of Moral Development." In describing stage six ("high moral behavior"), Mr. Jones said: "Undoubtedly, many in the clergy of all religions are on stage six. They have found God, and they follow in His ways. They are tolerant, because they know there are many ways to truth, and there are many ways to God."[3]

The *Ladies' Home Journal* asked Dr. Schlessinger if she thought that all roads lead to heaven whether you go to a synagogue or a mosque or church. Her response was: "The Jewish tradition says: The righteous shall inherit God's kingdom. Period. So, if there is an afterlife, I believe the righteous will be there. And I hope there's a tennis court."[4]

It becomes clear that Dr. Schlessinger believes that all religions and religious leaders should be considered equal in value as long as they are God-centered and encourage traditional Judeo-Christian ethics. After listening for many months to her, Sue Bohlin offered her assessment of Dr. Laura's welcoming attitude toward a wide variety of belief systems:

> Dr. Laura believes that all religions are equally expedient for establishing morality. If a young mother calls, looking for a religion in which to raise her children, Dr. Laura doesn't care if it's Hinduism or Islam or Presbyterianism, just as long as there is a religion. To her the issue is what works, or what seems to work, and most religions are the same to her in the area of shaping behavior.[5]

In a general sense, she indicates that we need God's law—particularly the Ten Commandments—as a basis for decision making. Rather than just going by our feelings, the Creator has given clear guidelines. (I recommend the reading of her fourth book, *The Ten Commandments: The Significance of God's Laws in Everyday Life.*) Dr. Laura offers this general assessment of various approaches to moral and ethical standards of conduct: ". . . basically it's biblical religious understanding. The Christian rules of behavior and the Islamic rules of behavior and the Jewish rules of behavior are actually not all that different."[6]

In reference to the religion of humanism, she reluctantly conceded the following while asking and answering her own question during a conversation with a caller: "Can a person be good without God? Well, if you follow the framework of God's rules and what good is—yeah—I guess so. But you've got to accept rules beyond your own definition of good. That's the tricky part."[7]

Dr. Schlessinger's open-mindedness in this regard leads her to adamantly deny any attempt to proselytize: "I'm very proud when people write to me that they have converted to Judaism because they have seen the beauty of it. But I don't proselytize."[8]

It should be noted that Dr. Laura is extremely fair in this regard. She shows genuine respect for everyone who calls regardless of his or her religious persuasion. The leading lady of talk radio welcomes born-again Christians along with agnostics. Catholics and Protestants. Jews and Gentiles. Muslims and Hindus.

However, she draws a line in the sand when it comes to atheism, humanism and the New Age movement. Here's why: These philosophies lack a fundamental belief in God. Her doctorate in physiology provided too many reasons to believe in a Supreme Being. Dr. Laura's commitment to Judaism and her firm belief in God's covenant with His chosen people simply cannot make room for a Godless existence. But still, she is gracious and willing to listen to those who do not believe in God.

George Gallup, president of the George H. Gallup International Institute, and the man behind the Gallup Poll, argues that America's generic approach to spirituality has diluted the concept of truly knowing and obeying God. He contends that the current popularity of religion does not necessarily indicate deep faith:

> We are in the most churched period of our entire history. Yet, while religion is broad, it is not very deep. God does not have primacy in most people's lives. People are moving toward a vague, free-floating and fuzzy spirituality which has no form.[9]

Mr. Gallup is right. It's all too vague. It's precariously free-floating. And it does lead to fuzzy spirituality. People are not getting closer to God. Rather, they are getting closer to themselves. It is humanism sugarcoated with God-talk. This is the pretense of religion, for it is utterly devoid of an actual, personal relationship with the Almighty.

Dr. Laura is to be commended for her intense search for a real relationship with God. During my interview with her, this came through in dramatic fashion. She is utterly sincere in her dedication to understanding God and Judaism.

Heaven on Earth

Dr. Schlessinger has some interesting views concerning the kingdom of God here on earth. Because of her uncertainty regarding an eternal heaven in an afterlife, what we make for ourselves in the present may, in her view, be all that we can expect. God's kingdom purpose for placing us here on earth as human beings, according to Dr. Laura, was stated in the interview with Andrew Cohen.

She refers to the Hebrew phrase *tikkun olam*, "perfect the world." Jews believe that we are all in partnership with God to make this world a better place. We were placed here to create a heaven on earth. When Cohen asked Dr. Schlessinger if there was anything humans could do to bring about this perfecting of the earth, she immediately replied: "Yes. It is by your actions. It is totally by your actions."[10]

The doctor proceeds to illustrate the need to obey the 613 commandments given to the Jews. For instance, we must visit the ill and take care of the needy. These are not optional. This is God's will. We must do them. She oversimplifies by comparing it to swinging the sledgehammer at the fair to make the weight go up and ring the bell. When the divine commandments are faithfully observed, the bell rings, and we have brought God's kingdom to earth. In Dr. Laura's words: "Everyone that does good gets us closer to God's kingdom on earth."[11]

It should be noted again that the emphasis in Dr. Laura's statements is on what human beings can do for God. By performing good deeds, we earn His kingdom. But in the Bible, we learn that humans beings need God to do something for us. We were lost and without hope, but the Creator came to us through His Son, Jesus. We can be redeemed only because of what He did for us.

Dr. Schlessinger acknowledges that the obligation everyone has to God is based on the fact that Jehovah said, "I am the LORD your God, who brought you out of Egypt, out of the land of slavery" (Exodus 20:2). She says:

> I came to learn that the Exodus experience was a story of redemption of a people from bondage into a covenant with God to bring to all peoples His character and desire for universal love and ethical behavior.[12]

The Bible agrees with this statement. But there's more. Jesus Christ claimed to be the very embodiment of God's character. As our lives are transformed by His power, we express the love of God and practice ethical behavior.

Hell on Earth

Dr. Laura evidently does not believe in a literal hell. When Mary Mohler asked the rather pointed question ("What about hell?") in *Ladies' Home Journal,* Dr. Laura responded: "Who needs future reference? What are the killing fields of Cambodia? Stalin's Russia? The Holocaust? We create hell right here. To me, the point of a righteous individual is to stand between the innocent and evil."[13]

Dr. Schlessinger has touched upon some rather cardinal doctrines of the Bible in this opening section of chapter 20. Dr. Billy Graham became famous for prefacing his comments with one simple phrase, "The Bible says." That is what I propose to offer in these closing pages. Here's what the Bible says. We must choose who we believe and who we follow.

Liar, Lunatic or Lord?

No religious founder or leader has ever made a claim like Jesus Christ. Some have claimed to be a spokesperson for God. Others have said that they were sent by the Creator to be examples for all humanity. But only one person has alleged to be equal to God Almighty. In fact, Jesus said: "I and the Father are one" (John 10:30), and "Anyone who has seen me has seen the Father" (14:9).

As if this were not fanatical enough, Christ also asserted that He was the one and only way to eternal life. In response to the question from an apostle with regard to finding the way to God and heaven, the Lord Jesus answered: "I am the way and the truth and the life. No one comes to the Father except through me" (14:6).

This is the most extreme and exclusive statement that has ever been made concerning the way to eternal life. If Christ told the truth, then there cannot be many ways to truth and God as Roger

Jones states in *The Dr. Laura Perspective.* Jesus excludes every other possible option for securing a right relationship with His Father and obtaining entrance into His eternal kingdom.

Because of her openness and respect for most religions, Dr. Laura would not criticize Christianity. She would never speak against Jesus Christ or demean Him in any specific way. She would probably say that He was a dynamic communicator. Dr. Laura is proud of His Jewish heritage, but because in Jewish theology the Messiah has not yet come, the Lord Jesus could not have been more than just an outstanding religious teacher.

Therefore, she would disagree with His most dramatic claim: that He was God's Son, the one and only Messiah. But is it possible that the Lord Jesus Christ was just a good moral teacher on the same level of Gandhi or Mohammed? If so, how do we interpret the extreme and adamant statements He made concerning His identity as "one with the Father"? Why would Jesus claim to be the one and only way to God?

C.S. Lewis responds to these inquiries with profound insight:

> I am trying here to prevent anyone saying the really foolish thing that people often say about Him: "I'm ready to accept Jesus as a great moral teacher, but I don't accept His claim to be God." That is the one thing we must not say. A man who was merely a man and said the sort of things Jesus said would not be a great moral teacher. He would either be a lunatic—on a level with a man who says he is a poached egg—or else he would be the Devil of Hell. You must make your choice. Either this man was, and is, the Son of God; or else a madman or something worse. You can shut Him up for a fool, you can spit at Him and kill Him as a demon; or you can fall at His feet and call Him Lord and God.

But let us not come with any patronizing nonsense about His being a great human teacher. He has not left that open to us. He did not intend to.[14]

Josh McDowell alliterated the thoughts in this paragraph by C.S. Lewis: "We must choose whether Christ was (and is) a liar, a lunatic, or the Lord of all."[15] If we conclude that Jesus was either a liar or a lunatic, we shouldn't even tell our children about Him. The Bible would then have to be regarded as a book of fairy tales and ethical ideals. But it would certainly not have or deserve any binding authority or preeminence in the lives of individuals or our society. Josh McDowell adds his thoughts to those of Mr. Lewis:

If, when Jesus made His claims He knew that He was not God, then He was lying. But, if He was a liar, then He was also a hypocrite because He told others to be honest, whatever the cost, while Himself teaching and living a colossal lie. And, more than that, He was a demon, because He told others to trust Him for their eternal destiny. If He could not back up His claims and knew it, then He was unspeakably evil. Lastly, He would also be a fool because it was His claims to being God that led to His crucifixion.[16]

However, when we accept Christ as the Lord of all, which He repeatedly claimed to be, we have immediately and irrevocably excluded every other religious system. It is simply impossible to concur with John 14:6 while at the same time making room for other beliefs. Either the Lord Jesus was telling the whole truth and nothing but the truth, or we are dealing with an extremely wicked and deceptive person.

This restrictive position is becoming less and less popular. Many people in churches today are backpedaling rapidly on this issue.

They are trying to find some way around the radical claims of Christ that would enable other sincere, religious people to find their own way to God. The alternative just seems so, well, intolerant and perhaps a tad arrogant.

But it is Jesus who proclaims that His way is a "narrow" one, and "only a few find it" (Matthew 7:14).

Let me be clear: This is not about one denomination or religion being the only way. It is about the person of Jesus Christ and who He claimed to be. It is about a personal relationship with Jesus Christ and how that can be obtained. Christians with various denominational labels are simply agreeing with what God has said through His Son and the Holy Spirit. We have chosen to stake our eternal future on the revolutionary claims of this One who claimed unequivocally to be the Son of God.

When asked the same question by *Ladies' Home Journal* as to whether or not "all roads lead to heaven," Anne Graham Lotz lovingly and boldly replied:

> I, too, believe that the righteous will inherit heaven, but not that all roads go there. Righteousness means to be right with God. We're made right with God through Christ. So I believe that all roads can lead you to the point that you find Christ. But the only way into heaven is through faith in Jesus Christ.[17]

Everyone cannot be right on this point. There are either many ways to truth and God or just one. The Bible-believing person must side with the claims of Christ.

A Prepared Place

Jesus stated in no uncertain terms that there will be a heaven:

"Do not let your hearts be troubled. Trust in God; trust also in me. In my Father's house are many rooms; if it were not so, I would have told you. I am going there to prepare a place for you. And if I go and prepare a place for you, I will come back and take you to be with me that you also may be where I am. You know the way to the place where I am going." (John 14:1-4)

This is a reference to the blessed hope of every person who has trusted Christ to be his or her Savior. Jesus is coming back for us! He will take us to heaven. It is described like this:

Then I saw a new heaven and a new earth, for the first heaven and the first earth had passed away, and there was no longer any sea. I saw the Holy City, the new Jerusalem, coming down out of heaven from God. . . . God himself will be with them and be their God. He will wipe every tear from their eyes. There will be no more death or mourning or crying or pain, for the old order of things has passed away.

He who was seated on the throne said, "I am making everything new!" Then he said, "Write this down, for these words are trustworthy and true." (Revelation 21:1-5)

This is no fairy tale. This is not merely an afterlife. Heaven is an actual location. It is as real as the room where you are sitting to read this book. It is a place prepared for people who are prepared—men, women, young people and children who are qualified for entrance to God's kingdom by their dependence on Jesus' sacrifice and righteousness.

No one will enter there based on his or her own merits. We can only gain entry to heaven through the work of Jesus Christ the Savior on our behalf.

A Hell to Shun

Another exceptionally clear teaching of the Scripture is in regard to the reality of eternal punishment in hell. Jesus spoke graphically about the horrors of the future location of those who ultimately reject the love and forgiveness which He offers. It's a story about two real people—Lazarus and a rich man. They both really died. And they both really went to their respective reward and punishment. The description is frightening far beyond the words used:

> In hell, where he [the rich man] was in torment, he looked up and saw Abraham far away, with Lazarus by his side. So he called to him, "Father Abraham, have pity on me and send Lazarus to dip the tip of his finger in water and cool my tongue, because I am in agony in this fire."
>
> But Abraham replied, "Son, remember that in your lifetime you received your good things, while Lazarus received bad things, but now he is comforted here and you are in agony. And besides all this, between us and you a great chasm has been fixed, so that those who want to go from here to you cannot, nor can anyone cross over from there to us." (Luke 16:23-26)

It must be repeated that if Christ was not telling the truth about hell in this terrifying passage, He is guilty of the worst kind of fraud. He would be responsible for unnecessarily invoking intense fear and dread about a place that does not even exist. Is this the kind of person that should be adored as a great moral teacher? Absolutely not! This would be like a cruel father who controls his children by threatening a visit from the bogeyman if they don't behave.

Christ spoke of a literal hell because it is an actual place. Those who do not have their names written in the Lamb's book of life will perish in separation from God for all eternity. John describes it this way at the end of the Revelation:

> Then I saw a great white throne and him who was seated on it. Earth and sky fled from his presence, and there was no place for them. And I saw the dead, great and small, standing before the throne, and books were opened. Another book was opened, which is the book of life. The dead were judged according to what they had done as recorded in the books. . . . If anyone's name was not found written in the book of life, he was thrown into the lake of fire. (Revelation 20:11-12, 15)

The very character and nature of God require a place like hell. Though He is a loving God, "not wanting anyone to perish" (2 Peter 3:9), Jehovah is also a just and righteous Creator. This is why Paul says that we should "[c]onsider therefore the kindness and sternness of God" (Romans 11:22). The Lord is not *either* kind or stern—His commitment to love and justice demands that He is *both*.

His holiness cannot tolerate even the hint of sinful rebellion. So this gracious God sent His Son to be the perfect sacrifice for our iniquities. By repenting of our sins and trusting in the righteousness of Jesus, we can escape the justified wrath of His Father.

"I don't believe in unconditional love—
period. That is insane."
—Dr. Laura[1]

Good News for Dr. Laura
—and You

ICONCLUDE THIS WRITING with some good news for Dr. Laura. It is also good news for you the reader. But before I get to that, I want to reiterate what I said in the opening part of the book. I have enormous respect for Dr. Laura Schlessinger. She is having a positive influence in many ways. In a society that has lost its moral compass, Dr. Laura is a guide back to the incredibly simple and sensible absolutes of Judeo-Christian ethics.

This radio talk-show host has denounced irresponsibility and instant gratification. She has held high the ideals of character, courage and conscience. Dr. Laura is an advocate of children—both the born and the unborn. With humor and wit, she reveals the clear differences between men and women, urging both sides to cherish and learn from the other. She boldly differentiates between love and lust. She openly attacks pornography, prostitution and premarital sex.

In short, Dr. Laura Schlessinger has been willing to take strong and sometimes unpopular positions on issues that our world says demand tolerance and open-mindedness. Most things are just two colors in the good doctor's world—black and white. There are very few shades of gray.

I suppose someone would be tempted to ask me this question: "Tom, after researching the life, the writings and the radio program of Dr. Schlessinger, and talking with her in person, would you recommend her radio program and her books?" Here's my unhesitating answer: Yes! Dr. Laura is "right on" most of the time. Much benefit can be derived from listening to her radio program and reading her books. God has given her unusual insight into many of the moral dilemmas that we face today. And we could all use a dose of her boldness.

Dr. Bill Hybels once said to a group of pastors, "I'm open to anything that doesn't compromise Scripture." In the same way, we can be open to what Dr. Laura has to offer. I have highlighted many positive stands she has taken which are fully endorsed by the Bible.

Also, in this book, I have tried to point out those areas where Dr. Schlessinger clearly deviates from the Bible. We cannot find common ground on these issues. But there is no need to throw the baby out with the bathwater. I have learned several good things from her books and by listening to *The Dr. Laura Show*. You will, too.

Morality without Redemption

The major struggle with Dr. Laura's program, books and other writings could be summarized like this: She offers "unredeemed morality." As the reader has noted, most of her positions are biblical. If the whole world listened to Dr. Schlessinger and followed her advice, our society could certainly boast of an improved morality. But it would still not be redeemed.

Dr. Laura can take things only so far. She offers no Redeemer. With no Redeemer, there cannot be any genuine grace, forgiveness or restoration. It's up to you and me to deal with past sin in the best way we can muster. And then we must somehow find the strength to deal with present and future temptation. For the most optimistic among us, this is a bleak scenario with very little lasting hope.

A man called Dr. Laura's show on June 10, 1998. He was struggling with homosexual desires even though he was married and had three children. She correctly chastised him for even giving consideration to leaving his family so that he could act out his fantasies with other men. The doctor reminded him that he had made a solemn vow and his feelings didn't really matter.

So what was he to do with his strong homosexual temptations? Dr. Laura advised that he should just "put them in a box." It was an obvious metaphor. She was telling him to ignore the feelings and concentrate on his commitment to his family. It was good advice, but it was inadequate.

This reminds me of a story my father used to tell. A communist was spouting forth the benefits of his ideology from a platform in a park. While pointing to an indigent man, he said, "Do you see that bum walking over there? I tell you, folks, communism can put a new suit on that man!" A Christian in the audience quickly grabbed the microphone and said, "Ladies and gentlemen, I tell you that Jesus Christ can put a new man in that suit!"

What Dr. Laura offers is to put a new suit on somebody. In other words, she can help people dress up the outward appearance. Put your feelings in a box. Do your best to cope with your sordid temptations. She cannot, and doesn't pretend to offer what is really needed—a change of heart! Only Jesus can do that.

For the man struggling with homosexual lust, it's not simply a matter of just putting his feelings in a box. Rather, he can cast himself at the feet of Christ, admitting that he has no power over his lustful temptation. And the Lord Jesus will give him the strength to say a firm "No!" and mean it. This battle with evil may not be a short one. Such a man has most likely developed sinful habits which have fueled the fire of his aberrant desire. But if he will confess his sin, he can be forgiven and placed morally right side up. Then day by day, moment by moment, he can lean upon the Savior for his strength.

How I thank God that Jesus Christ came to earth, lived a perfect life, died a sacrificial death and rose again in authoritative victory over sin, Satan and death. This changes everything.

And it leads us to the "good news."

The Messiah Has Come

Just listen to this: "The Messiah has already arrived!" This is good news for all of us! The "Anointed One" of God has been sent from the Father. No more searching. No more waiting. Jesus Christ is the one promised to the world by the prophet Isaiah:

> For to us a child is born,
>   to us a son is given,
>   and the government will be on his shoulders.
> And he will be called
>   Wonderful Counselor, Mighty God,
>   Everlasting Father, Prince of Peace.
> Of the increase of his government and peace
>   there will be no end.
> He will reign on David's throne
>   and over his kingdom,
> establishing and upholding it
>   with justice and righteousness
>   from that time on and forever.
> The zeal of the LORD Almighty
>   will accomplish this. (Isaiah 9:6-7)

When Jesus was talking with the Samaritan woman, she said: "I know that Messiah" (called Christ) "is coming. When he comes, he will explain everything to us" (John 4:25).

The Savior's reply caught her off guard: "I who speak to you am he" (4:26).

He is here! He is among us! What incredibly wonderful news!

Not only has our Messiah come, but He came for a specific purpose: "[T]he Son of Man did not come to be served, but to serve, and to give his life as a ransom for many" (Matthew 20:28).

The Lord Jesus was born to die for our sins. The blood of bulls and goats in the Old Testament was not sufficient to satisfy God's holiness. The good works of the Pharisees, scribes and chief priests in the New Testament fell short of Jehovah's lofty demands. Only one sacrifice was good enough—the blood of His only Son.

Paul described the complete adequacy of Christ's sacrifice this way:

> For what the law was powerless to do in that it was weakened by the sinful nature, God did by sending his own Son in the likeness of sinful man to be a sin offering. And so he condemned sin in sinful man, in order that the righteous requirements of the law might be fully met in us, who do not live according to the sinful nature but according to the Spirit. (Romans 8:3-4)

No one—including Tom Allen, Dr. Laura Schlessinger or you, the reader—can ultimately attain to God's standard of righteousness. We may try to scrupulously follow every single law that was ever devised in any religious system. But, like the Pharisees, we will fail miserably when it comes to matters of the heart. Those good works never wash away the stain of our sins. We will still be sinners who "fall short of the glory of God" (3:23) It just won't be good enough.

In fact, only one person ever has been good enough: Jesus Christ! This is why He was the perfect sacrifice for the sins of the whole world. This is why Jesus is the only One who can offer the grace, mercy and forgiveness which we so desperately need: "[W]e have one who has been tempted in every way, just as we are—yet was without sin. Let us then approach the throne of grace with confidence, so that we may receive mercy and find grace to help us in our time of need" (Hebrews 4:15-16).

Paul reminds us that our salvation is completely dependent on the Savior's grace:

> For it is by grace you have been saved, through faith—and this not from yourselves, it is the gift of God—not by works, so that no one can boast. For we are God's workmanship, created in Christ Jesus to do good works, which God prepared in advance for us to do. (Ephesians 2:8-10)

This text makes it exceptionally clear that even the good works we do emanate from Christ who is living within us. Thus, we cannot claim credit for our righteous behavior because it is not ours—it is His.

Yes! We have sinned. No! We cannot remedy the situation through any attempt at self-righteousness. But here is what we can count on: "[W]e have one who speaks to the Father in our defense—Jesus Christ, the Righteous One. He is the atoning sacrifice for our sins, and not only for ours but also for the sins of the whole world" (1 John 2:1-2).

This is very good news indeed! The Lord Jesus Christ has done something for us that we could not do for ourselves. He has made it possible for us to be declared "righteous" in the presence of His Father! My dad use to pull out a white handkerchief and place it over a black comb. It was an illustration of how God looks upon us when we are in Christ. Jehovah sees the wonderful white purity of His Son—not the darkness of our sin. In the words of the apostle Paul: "God made him who had no sin to be sin for us, so that in him we might become the righteousness of God" (2 Corinthians 5:21). This is unconditional love. We can count on it because "God demonstrates his own love for us in this: While we were still sinners, Christ died for us" (Romans 5:8).

Knowing all about the intimate details of our many failures, God still loves you and me! Remarkable? Yes! Unbelievable? Of course! But it's true. Jesus has taken our sins upon Himself and given us His righteousness.

The Messiah Has Provided Eternal Life

The Messiah has come. He has paid the full penalty for all of our sins so that we can have a righteous standing before God. Jesus, our Messiah, also made these incredible promises:

> "For God so loved the world that he gave his one and only Son, that whoever believes in him shall not perish but have eternal life." (John 3:16)

> "[W]hoever lives and believes in me will never die." (11:26)

The apostle John offered these words of assurance:

> I write these things to you who believe in the name of the Son of God so that you may know that you have eternal life. . . . We know also that the Son of God has come and has given us understanding, so that we may know him who is true. And we are in him who is true—even in his Son Jesus Christ. He is the true God and eternal life. (1 John 5:13, 20)

Those of us who turn from our sins and trust Christ to be our Savior are guaranteed eternal life. This is no mere hope. Heaven is not only a theological concept. I am talking about a place that is even more real than the chair in which you are sitting right now. And it cannot be earned. Eternal life is a gift from God which is entirely based on the merits of Jesus Christ and His righteousness (Ephesians 2:8-9).

"Who Do You Say I Am?"

> Jesus and his disciples went on to the villages around Caesarea Philippi. On the way he asked them, "Who do people say I am?"
> They replied: "Some say John the Baptist; others say Elijah; and still others, one of the prophets."
> "But what about you?" he asked. "Who do you say I am?"
> Peter answered, "You are the Christ." (Mark 8:27-29)

I conclude this book with the same question for each reader: "Who do you say that Christ is?" Is He a "liar" who gets His kicks from promising things He can never deliver? Would "lunatic" fit your description of Jesus because of His outlandish claims? Or is He "Lord of all"?

There is no single inquiry of greater consequence both in this world and the world to come. Consider the possible end results.

Let's assume that many open-minded people are right in their contention that there is really no difference between religions because they all eventually lead to God.

There is no hell except that which we make for ourselves in this world by perpetuating evil. There is no heaven save that which we create for ourselves right here and now by our righteous acts.

If this is all true, then devoted Christians have lost nothing as followers of Christ. We have enjoyed the fruit of living according to Judeo-Christian ethics. And, as Dr. Laura has said, "Morality is its own reward."

But what if Jesus Christ is exactly who He said He is? What if He is indeed the only way to God and eternal life as He claimed to be? What if there really are places called heaven and hell? And let's say it is true that only those who have trusted in Christ as their Savior will be able to enter heaven on His merits, whereas all others will be separated from God forever in the torments of hell?

The consequences for being wrong about this are—to put it mildly—catastrophic.

Accepting God's Gift

What makes the most sense is to believe on the Lord Jesus Christ and accept the good news! Then we can pursue a righteous life that is based on the work of Jesus in us rather than what we can do to please Him. We will renounce all attempts to manufacture our own self-righteousness because that no longer matters. Our pursuit of holiness in character and conduct becomes a response to His grace.

So how does one become a Christian and secure the promise of eternal life?

We simply decide to become a follower of Jesus Christ. Then we can pray a simple prayer. We confess our sinfulness, call upon God's mercy and accept the free gift of God's salvation through His Son. "[E]veryone who calls on the name of the Lord will be saved" (Acts 2:21).

Introduction

1. "Dr. Morality," *Leadership Journal*, (Winter, 1998), 114.
2. *The Late, Late Show with Tom Snyder*, CBS-TV, May 6, 1998.
3. "Dr. Laura Cuts Thru Hot Air," by Colleen Gibbs, *Radio Guide USA*, taken from the Internet, www5.electriciti.com/vvdesign/benj/djprofile/laura.html, 2.

Part 1: Meet Dr. Laura

Chapter 1—Good Things Come in Small Packages

1. Joannie M. Schrof, "No Whining!", *U.S. News & World Report*, July 14, 1997, 48.
2. Laura Schlessinger, *Ten Stupid Things Women Do to Mess Up Their Lives* (New York: Harper Collins, 1995), 231.
3. "About Dr. Laura," taken from the Internet, www. drlaura.com, 2.
4. Schlessinger, *Ten Stupid Things Women Do to Mess Up Their Lives*, 231.
5. Andrea Adelson, "A Dash Past Rush?", *The New York Times*, April 13, 1998, C-7.
6. *The Late, Late Show with Tom Snyder*, CBS-TV, May 6, 1998.
7. "Dr. Laura Cuts Thru Hot Air," by Colleen Gibbs, *Radio Guide USA*, taken from the Internet, www5.electriciti.com/vvdesign/benj/djprofile/laura.html, 2.
8. Schrof, "No Whining!", 51.
9. "Dr. Morality," *Leadership Journal* (Winter, 1998), 115.
10. Laura Schlessinger, *How Could You Do That?!* (New York: HarperCollins, 1996), 4-5.
11. Schlessinger, *Ten Stupid Things Women Do to Mess Up Their Lives*, 60.
12. Ibid., 215.
13. Laura Schlessinger, *Ten Stupid Things Men Do to Mess Up Their Lives* (New York: HarperCollins, 1997), 140.
14. Schlessinger, *How Could You Do That?!,* 40-41.

15. Philip V. Brennan, Jr., "How Did Radio's Dr. Laura Get Herself Compared to St. Thomas Aquinas?", Capitol Research Center, taken from the Internet, www.policyreview.com/crc/cw/cw-0597.html, May, 1997.

16. Schlessinger, *How Could You Do That?!*, 54.

17. Schlessinger, *Ten Stupid Things Women Do, 232.*

18. Laura Schlessinger, "What Is a Well-Lived Life?", *Parade* (March 15, 1998), 5.

19. Suzanne F. Singer, "Dr. Laura—'National Mommy' and Jewish Priest," *Moment* (April, 1997), 68.

20. Schlessinger, *Ten Stupid Things Women Do,* 231.

21. Schlessinger, "What Is a Well-Lived Life?", 4.

22. Schlessinger, *Ten Stupid Things Men Do,* from cover flap on cloth edition.

23. *The Dr. Laura Show*, taped from KSTP AM 1500 (Minneapolis, MN, June 30, 1998).

Chapter 2—A Prophetess without Honor

1. Joannie M. Schrof, "No Whining!", *U.S. News & World Report,* July 14, 1997, 48.

2. Ibid.

3. Ted and Virginia Byfield, "Orthodoxy," *Alberta Report* (Internet Edition, August 4, 1997), 2.

4. Amy Bernstein, "Dr. Laura's Moral Health Show," *U.S. News & World Report* (Internet Edition, April 29, 1996), 2.

5. Doris Quan, "Counseling America," taken from the Internet, www.msnbc.com, 3.

6. Kristin Tillotson, "Doctor, Heal Thyself!" *Star Tribune* (Minneapolis, MN, January 4, 1998), 9F.

7. *Star Tribune*, Minneapolis, MN, January 11, 1998, 9F.

8. Quan, "Counseling America," 3.

9. Suzanne F. Singer, "Dr. Laura—'National Mommy' and Jewish Priest," *Moment* (April, 1997), 67, and Pythia Peay, "Soundbites from a Talk Show Moralist," *Religious News Digest*, June 23, 1996.

10. Carolyn Poirot, "Are Radio Shrinks on the Right Wavelength?", *Fort Worth Star-Telegram,* January 13, 1997.

11. "Dr. Laura's Monologue," taken from the Internet, www.drlaura.com (January 8, 1998).

12. Ibid.

13. Joan Austin, "Comments" (E-mail commentary posted on the Internet, August 4, 1997).

14. Philip V. Brennan, Jr., "How Did Radio's Dr. Laura Get Herself Compared to St. Thomas Aquinas?", Capitol Research Center, taken from the Internet, www.policy-review.com/crc/cw/cw-0597.html, May, 1997.

15. Pythia Peay, "Soundbites from a Talk Show Moralist," *Religious News Digest,* June 23, 1996.

16. Poirot, "Are Radio Shrinks."

17. Ibid.

18. Ibid.

19. Ibid.

20. Schrof, "No Whining!", 50.

21. Taken from the Internet, www.wmcstations.com/am790/browne.htm.

22. Taken from the Internet, www.achilles.net/guy/laura/m33.htm.

23. Laura Berman, "Dr. Laura, Don't Blame Writers for Your Rude Behavior," *The Detroit News* (March 20, 1997).

24. USA Today, October 26, 1998, p. D1.

25. Rabbi Peter Grumbacher, "Dr. Laura: The 'Theologian' of the Days of Awe," *The Dr. Laura Perspective* (Volume 3, Issue 5, March, 1998), 5.

Part 2: Human Development

Chapter 3—The Age of the Victim

1. Martin E.P. Seligman and Roger Weissberg, "Less Benignly, It Can Stir Violence, Too," *USA Today,* May 27, 1998, 15a.

2. Laura Schlessinger, *Ten Stupid Things Women Do to Mess Up Their Lives* (New York: HarperCollins, 1995), xviii (introduction).

3. Laura Schlessinger, *How Could You Do That?!* (New York: HarperCollins, 1996), 8-9.

4. Ibid., 2-3.

5. Ibid.

6. Ibid.

7. Ibid., 9.

8. Ibid.

9. "Dr. Laura," *Star Tribune* (Minneapolis, MN, February 15, 1998), E6.

10. Ibid.

11. Schlessinger, *How Could You Do That?!,* 253-254.

12. Ibid., 215.

13. "Dr. Morality," *Leadership Journal* (Winter, 1998), 115.

14. *NBC News This Week with Sam Donaldson and Cokie Roberts,* March 29, 1998.

15. Schlessinger, *How Could You Do That?!,* 171.

16. Joannie M. Schrof, "No Whining!", *U.S. News & World Report,* July 14, 1997, 50.

Chapter 4—When No One Else Is Looking

1. Laura Schlessinger, *How Could You Do That?!* (New York: HarperCollins, 1996), 1.
2. Ibid., 5.
3. Ibid., 10.
4. Joannie M. Schrof, "No Whining!", *U.S. News & World Report,* July 14, 1997, 50.
5. Schlessinger, *How Could You Do That?!,* 208.
6. Ibid., 192-194.
7. Ibid.
8. Ibid., 5.
9. Ibid., 10-11.
10. "Dr. Laura," *Star Tribune* (Minneapolis, MN, February 15, 1998), E6.
11. Schlessinger, *How Could You Do That?!,* 12.
12. Ibid.
13. Ibid., 10.

Chapter 5—What Broth Is to Soup

1. Laura Schlessinger, *How Could You Do That?* (New York: HarperCollins, 1996), 13.
2. Ibid.
3. Ibid.
4. Ibid., 64-91.

Chapter 6—Where's Your Conscience?

1. Laura Schlessinger, *How Could You Do That?* (New York: HarperCollins, 1996), 26.
2. Ibid., 6.
3. Ibid., 25.
4. Ibid., 15.
5. Ibid.
6. Ibid.
7. Ibid., 17.
8. Ibid., 15.
9. Ibid.

10. *The Dr. Laura Show*, taped from KSTP AM 1500 (Minneapolis, MN, April 21, 1998).
11. "Dr. Laura," *Star Tribune* (Minneapolis, MN, May 24, 1998), E9.
12. Joannie M. Schrof, "No Whining!", *U.S. News & World Report,* July 14, 1997, 55.
13. *The Dr. Laura Show*, taped from KSTP AM 1500 (Minneapolis, MN, June 1, 1998).
14. Ibid., June 19, 1998.
15. Mark Fackler and Christopher Bunn, "Is It Ever Right to Do Wrong?", *Discipleship Journal* (Issue 104, 1998), 40.
16. "Dr. Laura," *Star Tribune* (Minneapolis, MN, May 31, 1998), E7.
17. Ibid., May 10, 1998, E7.

Chapter 7—Delayed Gratification

1. Laura Schlessinger, *How Could You Do That?* (New York: HarperCollins, 1996), 26.
2. Ibid., 35.
3. Ibid., 35-36.
4. Ibid., 227.
5. Ibid., 16-17.
6. Ibid., 97.
7. Ibid., 149-150.
8. Ibid., 124-125.
9. Ibid., 186.
10. Ibid., 57.

Part 3: Issues of the Id

Chapter 8—New Attitude

1. Laura Schlessinger, *How Could You Do That?* (New York: HarperCollins, 1996), 5.
2. Chris Mruk, *Self-Esteem: Research, Theory, and Practice* (New York: Springer Publishing Company, Inc., 1995), 135.
3. Laura Schlessinger, *Ten Stupid Things Women Do to Mess Up Their Lives* (New York, New York: HarperCollins, 1995), 140-141.
4. Ibid.
5. Ibid., 10.
6. Ibid., 57.
7. Ibid., 217.
8. Ibid., 21.

9. Ibid., 12.
10. Ibid., 40-41.
11. Ibid., 196.
12. Charles Wesley, "And Can It Be That I Should Gain," verse 3, *Hymns of the Christian Life* (Camp Hill, PA: Christian Publications, 1992), 104.
13. Schlessinger, *How Could You Do That?!*, 93.

Chapter 9—You and Only You

1. Laura Schlessinger, *Ten Stupid Things Women Do to Mess Up Their Lives* (New York: HarperCollins, 1995), 94.
2. "Dr. Morality," *Leadership Journal* (Winter, 1998), 113-114.
3. Laura Schlessinger, *How Could You Do That?* (New York: HarperCollins, 1996), 22.
4. Ibid., 269.
5. Schlessinger, *Ten Stupid Things Women Do,* 52.
6. Ibid., 59.
7. Schlessinger, *How Could You Do That?!,* 152.
8. David Johnson with Tom Allen, *Joy Comes in the Mourning* (Camp Hill, PA: Christian Publications, Inc., 1998), 18.
9. Joel Belz, "Dr. Laura's Static," *World Magazine* (May 9, 1998), 5.

Part 4: Marriage and Family Matters

Chapter 10—Stay At Home, Mom (or Dad)

1. Suzanne F. Singer, "Dr. Laura—'National Mommy' and Jewish Priest," *Moment* (April, 1997), 68.
2. Laura Schlessinger, *Ten Stupid Things Women Do to Mess Up Their Lives* (New York: HarperCollins, 1995), 223-224.
3. Ibid., 224.
4. Laura Schlessinger, *Ten Stupid Things Men Do to Mess Up Their Lives* (New York: HarperCollins, 1997), 155.
5. Laura Schlessinger, *How Could You Do That?!* (New York: HarperCollins, 1996), 155.
6. Schlessinger, *Ten Stupid Things Men Do,* 63.
7. Ibid., 64.
8. Ibid.
9. Schlessinger, *How Could You Do That?!,* 93.
10. Joannie M. Schrof, "No Whining!", *U.S. News & World Report,* July 14, 1997, 54.
11. Schlessinger, *How Could You Do That?!,* 92-93.

12. Ibid., 174.
13. Ibid., 243.
14. Ibid.

Chapter 11—The Unformed Body

1. Laura Schlessinger, *Ten Stupid Things Men Do to Mess Up Their Lives* (New York: HarperCollins, 1997), 133.
2. "Dr. Morality," *Leadership Journal* (Winter, 1998), 113.
3. Laura Schlessinger, *How Could You Do That?* (New York: HarperCollins, 1996), 14.
4. Ibid., 53.
5. Sue Bohlin, "Why Dr. Laura Is (Usually) Right," taken from Probe Ministries on the Internet, www.probe.org/ docs/drlaura.html, (January 23, 1998), 5.
6. Schlessinger, *Ten Stupid Things Men Do,* 134.
7. Schlessinger, *How Could You Do That?!,* 82-83.
8. Ibid., 170-171.
9. Schlessinger, *Ten Stupid Things Men Do,* 138.

Chapter 12—For the Sake of the Children

1. Laura Schlessinger, *Ten Stupid Things Women Do to Mess Up Their Lives* (New York: HarperCollins, 1995), 160-161.
2. Joannie M. Schrof, "No Whining!", *U.S. News & World Report,* July 14, 1997, 54.
3. Schlessinger, *Ten Stupid Things Women Do,* 155.
4. Ibid., 172-173.
5. Ibid., 159.
6. Laura Schlessinger, *How Could You Do That?* (New York: HarperCollins, 1996), 222-223.
7. Laura Schlessinger, *Ten Stupid Things Men Do to Mess Up Their Lives* (New York: HarperCollins, 1997), 217.
8. Ibid., 219-220.
9. Ibid., 232.
10. Ibid., 231.
11. "Dr. Laura," *Star Tribune* (Minneapolis, MN, June 28, 1998), E7.

Chapter 13—Men Are from Jupiter, Women Are from Saturn

1. Laura Schlessinger, *Ten Stupid Things Men Do to Mess Up Their Lives* (New York: HarperCollins, 1997), 299.
2. Ibid., 57.
3. Ibid., 2.

4. Ibid., 32-33.
5. Ibid., 121.
6. Ibid., xii (introduction).
7. Ibid., xiii (introduction), 33.
8. Ibid., 34.
9. Laura Schlessinger, *Ten Stupid Things Women Do to Mess Up Their Lives* (New York: HarperCollins, 1995), 5-6.
10. Ibid., 7.
11. Ibid., 34.
12. Ibid., 167.
13. Ibid., 39.
14. Ibid., 23-24.
15. Ibid., 6.
16. Schlessinger, *Ten Stupid Things Men Do,* 35.
17. Ibid., 37.
18. Ibid., 114.

Part 5: Sexual Mores

Chapter 14 —Sex vs. Love

1. Laura Schlessinger, *Ten Stupid Things Women Do to Mess Up Their Lives* (New York: HarperCollins, 1995), 78.
2. Laura Schlessinger, *How Could You Do That?!* (New York: HarperCollins, 1996), 226.
3. Laura Schlessinger, *Ten Stupid Things Men Do to Mess Up Their Lives* (New York: HarperCollins, 1997), 143.
4. Schlessinger, *Ten Stupid Things Women Do,* 81.
5. Ibid., 66.
6. Schlessinger, *Ten Stupid Things Men Do,* 207.
7. Ibid., 126.
8. Schlessinger, *How Could You Do That?!,* 199-200.
9. Schlessinger, *Ten Stupid Things Men Do,* 129.

Chapter 15—Adam and Steve

1. Arsenio Orteza, "Talk Radio: I am my country's mom," *World on the Web* (August 9, 1997, Volume 12, Number 14), 3. (Taken from the Internet, www.worldmag.com, March 4, 1998.)
2. Michael Van Essen, "A Pound of Cure." *The Dr. Laura Perspective* (Volume 3, Number 1, November, 1997), 10.

3. Laura Schlessinger, *Ten Stupid Things Women Do to Mess Up Their Lives* (New York: HarperCollins, 1995), 58-59.

4. Laura Schlessinger, *How Could You Do That?!* (New York: HarperCollins, 1996), 244-245.

5. Ibid., 245-246.

6. Sue Bohlin, "Why Dr. Laura Is (Usually) Right," taken from Probe Ministries on the Internet, www.probe.org/docs/ drlaura.html, January 23, 1998.

7. *The Dr. Laura Show*, taped from KSTP AM 1500 (Minneapolis, MN, March 24, 1998).

8. Joannie M. Schrof, "No Whining!", *U.S. News & World Report*, July 14, 1997, 55.

9. "Excerpts from Anglican Statement," Associated Press, August 6, 1998.

10. *The Dr. Laura Show,* August 6, 1998. (Transcript provided by Dr. Laura Schlessinger.)

Chapter 16—Food for the Eyes—Starvation for the Soul

1. Laura Schlessinger, *Ten Stupid Things Men Do to Mess Up Their Lives* (New York: HarperCollins, 1997), 147.

2. Ibid.

3. Ibid., 147-148.

4. Ibid., 148.

5. Ibid., 148-149.

6. Ibid., 148.

7. Ibid.

8. Ibid., 149.

9. Ibid.

Chapter 17—Shacking Up

1. "Dr. Morality," *Leadership Journal* (Winter, 1998), 113.

2. "Dr. Laura's Monologue," taken from the Internet, www.drlaura.com (February 12, 1998), 4-5.

3. "Dr. Laura," *Star Tribune* (Minneapolis, MN, March 1, 1998).

4. Laura Schlessinger, *How Could You Do That?!* (New York: HarperCollins, 1996), 154.

5. Ibid., 20.

6. Laura Schlessinger, *Ten Stupid Things Women Do to Mess Up Their Lives* (New York: HarperCollins, 1995), 91.

7. "Dr. Laura's On-Line Column," taken from the Internet, www.drlaura.com (February 12, 1998), 2-3.

8. Laura Schlessinger, *Ten Stupid Things Men Do to Mess Up Their Lives* (New York: HarperCollins, 1997), 158.

9. Schlessinger, *Ten Stupid Things Women Do,* 95.

10. Ibid., 91-92.

11. Schlessinger, *Ten Stupid Things Men Do,* 149-150.

12. Schlessinger, *How Could You Do That?!,* 147-148.

13. Schlessinger, *Ten Stupid Things Men Do,* 39.

14. Ibid., 122.

15. Schlessinger, *How Could You Do That?!,* 20-21.

16. Schlessinger, *Ten Stupid Things Men Do,* 136.

17. Schlessinger, *How Could You Do That?!,* 33.

Part 6: Spirituality

Chapter 18—Inherently Neutral

1. Laura Schlessinger, *How Could You Do That?* (New York: HarperCollins, 1996), 185.

2. Laura Schlessinger, *Ten Stupid Things Men Do to Mess Up Their Lives* (New York: HarperCollins, 1997), 272, 300.

3. Andrew Cohen, "What Is Enlightenment?" (Number 12), taken from the Internet, www.moksha.com, 12.

4. Ibid.

5. *USA Today,* March 25, 1998, 1A.

6. *ABC News This Week with Sam Donaldson and Cokie Roberts,* March 29, 1998.

7. *The Dr. Laura Show,* taped from KSTP AM 1500 (Minneapolis, MN, May 6, 1998).

8. *USA Today,* March 25, 1998, 1A.

9. Brian Doherty, "Blame Those Who Pull the Trigger," *Milwaukee Journal Sentinel,* May 31, 1998, 1J.

Chapter 19—To the Unknowable (?) God

1. Andrew Cohen, "What Is Enlightenment?" (Number 12), taken from the Internet, www.moksha.com.

2. Ibid., 5-6.

3. Ibid., 14.

4. Ibid., 15.

5. Mary Mohler, "Are There Really Angels?" *Ladies' Home Journal,* April, 1998, 40.

6. Ibid., 42.

7. Ibid.

8. Suzanne F. Singer, "Dr. Laura—'National Mommy' and Jewish Priest," *Moment* (April, 1997), 57.

9. Ibid.

10. Mohler, "Are There Really Angels?", 46.

11. Ibid., 42.

Chapter 20—Many Ways to Truth and God?

1. Laura Schlessinger, "What Is a Well-lived Life?" *Parade* (March 15, 1998), 5.

2. *The Dr. Laura Show*, taped from KSTP AM 1500 (Minneapolis, MN, March 23, 1998).

3. Roger D. Jones, "The 6 Stages of Moral Development," *The Dr. Laura Perspective* (Volume 3, Issue 5, March, 1998), 12.

4. Mary Mohler, "Are There Really Angels?" *Ladies' Home Journal,* April, 1998, 43.

5. Sue Bohlin, "Why Dr. Laura Is (Usually) Right," taken from Probe Ministries on the Internet, www.probe.org/docs/drlaura.html (January 23, 1998), 6.

6. Andrew Cohen, "What Is Enlightenment?" (Number 12), taken from the Internet, www.moksha.com, 12.

7. *The Dr. Laura Show*, taped from KSTP AM 1500 (Minneapolis, MN, March 17, 1998).

8. Suzanne F. Singer, "Dr. Laura—'National Mommy' and Jewish Priest," *Moment* (April, 1997), 70.

9. "Pollster calls U.S. religious life 'superficial'," (Associated Press), *Star Tribune* (Minneapolis, MN, May 23, 1998), B7.

10. Cohen, "What Is Enlightenment?", 13-14.

11. Ibid., 14.

12. Laura Schlessinger and Rabbi Stewart Vogel, *The Ten Commandments: The Significance of God's Laws in Everyday Life* (New York: HarperCollins Publishers, Inc., 1998), xv.

13. Mary Mohler, "Are There Really Angels?", April, 1998, 43.

14. C.S. Lewis, *Mere Christianity* (New York: Macmillan Publishing Company, 1960), 41.

15. Josh McDowell, *Evidence That Demands a Verdict* Vol. 1 (San Bernadino, CA: Campus Crusade for Christ, 1972), 107.

16. Ibid., 109.

17. Mohler, "Are There Really Angels?", 43.

Epilogue

1. *The Dr. Laura Show*, taped from KSTP AM 1500 (Minneapolis, MN, June 19, 1998).

Books

Johnson, David and Tom Allen. *Joy Comes in the Mourning.* Camp Hill, Pennsylvania: Christian Publications, Inc., 1998.

Lewis, C.S. *Mere Christianity.* New York: Macmillan Publishing Company, 1960.

McDowell, Josh. *Evidence That Demands A Verdict,* Vol. 1. San Bernadino, California: Campus Crusade for Christ, 1972.

Mruk, Chris. *Self-Esteem: Research, Theory, and Practice.* New York, New York: Springer Publishing Company, Inc., 1995.

Schlessinger, Laura. *How Could You Do That?* New York: HarperCollins, 1996.

_____. *Ten Stupid Things Men Do to Mess Up Their Lives.* New York: HarperCollins, 1997.

_____. *Ten Stupid Things Women Do to Mess Up Their Lives.* New York: HarperCollins, 1995.

Schlessinger, Laura, and Vogel, Stewart. *The Ten Commandments: The Significance of God's Laws in Everyday Life.* New York: HarperCollins, 1998.

Major Magazine Articles

Bohlin, Sue. "Why Dr. Laura Is (Usually) Right," Probe Ministries. January 23, 1998. (Internet: www.probe.org/docs/ drlaura.html).

Cohen, Andrew. "What Is Enlightenment?" (Number 12). (Internet: www.moksha.com).

"Dr. Morality." *Leadership Journal.* Carol Stream, Illinois, Winter 1998.

Jones, Roger D. "The 6 Stages of Moral Development." *The Dr. Laura Perspective,* Volume 3, Issue 5, March 1998.

Mohler, Mary. "Are There Really Angels?" *Ladies Home Journal.* April, 1998.

Schlessinger, Laura. "What Is A Well-lived Life?" *Parade magazine.* March 15, 1998.

Schrof, Joannie M. "No Whining!" *U.S. News & World Report,* July 14, 1997.

Singer, Suzanne F. "Dr. Laura—'National Mommy' and Jewish Priest." *Moment.* Red Oak, Iowa. April, 1997.

Van Essen, Michael. ". . . A Pound of Cure." *The Dr. Laura Perspective,* Volume 3, Number 1, November, 1997.

Important Internet Websites

www.drlaura.com

www.moksha.com

www.probe.org/docs/drlaura.html

www.worldmag.com

Television Shows

ABC News This Week with Sam Donaldson and Cokie Roberts, ABC, March 29, 1998.

Larry King Live! CNN, April 22, 1998.

The Late, Late Show with Tom Snyder, CBS, May 6, 1998.

Radio Station

KSTP AM 1500, Minneapolis, Minnesota.

Other Books by Tom Allen

Congregations in Conflict

I Wish You Could Meet My Mom and Dad

Rock 'n Roll, the Bible and the Mind

*10 Foolish Things Christians Do
to Stunt Their Growth*

Joy Comes in the Mourning (with David Johnson)

Booklets by Tom Allen

"Spiritual Leadership Beings at Home"

"Let Him That Is without Sin . . ."